Table of Contents

List of Tables

Survey of Employer Perspectives on the Employment of People with Disabilities

Technical Report
November 2008

EXECUTIVE SUMMARY

The U.S. Department of Labor, Office of Disability Employment Policy (ODEP), conducted the 2008 Survey of Employer Perspectives on the Employment of People with Disabilities. The objective of this nationally representative survey was to inform the development and promotion of policy and practice by comparing employer perspectives across various industries and within companies of varying sizes. ODEP will use the data from this survey to formulate targeted strategies and policies for increasing employment opportunities for people with disabilities. This survey emphasized current attitudes and practices of employers in 12 industry sectors, including some high growth industries as projected by the Bureau of Labor Statistics (BLS).

The majority of statistics on the employment of people with disabilities are derived from nationally representative surveys, such as the Survey of Income and Program Participation, American Community Survey, National Health Interview Survey, and soon the Current Population Survey. However, there were no comprehensive surveys examining the employer side of issues related to recruiting, hiring, advancing and retaining people with disabilities. This 2008 ODEP Survey of Employer Perspectives on the Employment of People with Disabilities was designed to provide a source of nationally representative statistics on the employment of people with disabilities from the perspective of employers.

ODEP conducted a 15-minute telephone survey of a representative sample of senior executives representing 12 industries by company size: small (5-14 employees), medium (15-249 employees), and large companies (250 or more employees). The industries are:

1. Construction
2. Wholesale trade
3. Retail trade
4. Transportation and warehousing
5. Information
6. Financial activities
7. Professional and business services
8. Education and health services
9. Leisure and hospitality
10. Other services: establishments in this sector are primarily engaged in activities, such as equipment and machinery repairing, promoting or administering religious activities, grant making, advocacy, and providing dry cleaning and laundry services, personal care services, death care services, pet care services, photofinishing services, temporary parking services, and dating services.
11. State and local government
12. Manufacturing

Interviewing was conducted from February through June 2008. Interviews were completed with 3,797 respondents, for a response rate of 51.4 percent. The 3,797 companies in the sample represent 2,469,000 companies.

The strength of this survey is the ability to examine patterns by company size and industry. Results are provided for all companies and separately by company size and by three broad industry types. These three broad industry types follow the super-sectors of the North American Industry Classification System (NAICS). Goods-producing industries include construction and manufacturing. Service-producing industries include retail trade, wholesale trade, transportation/warehousing, leisure/hospitality, education/health, information, professional, finance, and other services. Public administration is its own super-sector consisting of establishments of federal, state, and local government agencies that administer, oversee, and manage public programs and have executive, legislative, or judicial authority over other institutions within a given area. The statistics in this report are calculated using sample weights.

Key findings are:

Employing people with disabilities

- Among companies in the United States, 471,562 companies (19.1 percent) report employing people with disabilities.
- Among small companies (employing 5 to 14 people), 10.7 percent report employing people with disabilities, while 22.6 percent of medium-sized companies (employing 15 to 249 employees) and 53.1 percent of large companies (employing 250 or more employees) report employing people with disabilities.

Recruiting people with disabilities

- 326,721 companies (13.6 percent) report that they actively recruit people with disabilities.
- Larger companies are more likely to actively recruit people with disabilities (33.8 percent) than smaller companies (7.8 percent).
- In absolute numbers, there are more mid-sized companies (164,460) recruiting people with disabilities than small (96,052) and large companies (66,209).
- Public administration organizations are more likely to actively recruit than their private sector counterparts.
- Among private sector companies, those in service-producing industries are more likely to actively recruit than those in goods-producing industries. Service-producing industries have the largest number of employers that actively recruit.

Persuading companies to recruit people with disabilities

- When asked about the type of information that would persuade them to recruit people with a disability, companies that do not actively recruit cited information about performance, productivity, and how hiring people with disabilities can benefit a company's bottom line as the most persuasive information, while information about cost is the least persuasive.
- Information on satisfactory job performance and how hiring people with disabilities can increase a company's productivity are cited by small and medium-sized company as most persuasive.

- Large companies are more likely to be persuaded by information that is supported by statistics or research.

Hiring people with disabilities

- 215,344 companies (8.7 percent) report having hired people with disabilities in the past 12 months.
- Large companies are more likely to report having hired a person with disabilities in the past 12 months (32.6 percent) compared to medium-sized companies at 8 percent.
- The nature of the work being such that it cannot be effectively performed by a person with a disability is cited as a hiring challenge by 72.6 percent of all companies. Attitudes of co-workers or supervisors are the least frequently cited challenges. Health care costs, workers compensation costs and fear of litigation are more challenging for small and medium companies than for large companies.
- The cost of employing people with disabilities and the belief that workers with disabilities lack the skills and experience necessary are the most often cited concerns for small and mid-sized companies, while supervisor uncertainty about how to take disciplinary action is cited most often for large companies.

Advancing Employees with Disabilities

- For companies that currently employ people with disabilities, the cost of accommodation and lack of advancement potential are the top two challenges to advancing employees with disabilities, regardless of company size, far surpassing attitudes of customers, co-workers or supervisors.

Retaining Employees with Disabilities

- For companies that currently employ people with disabilities, finding ways to return employees to work after the onset of a disability is the number one challenge for medium and large companies.
- For companies that currently employ people with disabilities, visible commitment from top management is an important strategy in retaining people with disabilities. Small and mid-sized companies are more likely to cite employer tax credits as a retention strategy than are large companies. Large companies most often cite mentoring as the top strategy for retention.

Knowledge of One-Stop Career Centers

- One-Stop Career Centers are designed to provide a full range of assistance to job seekers and employers in one location. Established under the Workforce Investment Act, the centers offer training referrals, career counseling, job listings, and other employment-related services. Twenty-five percent of employers are aware of local One-Stop Career Centers. Large companies (42.6 percent) and employers in public administration (38.1 percent) are more likely to know of local One-Stop Career Centers. Within the private sector, the proportion of employers in goods-producing industries aware of One-Stop services (25.5 percent) is roughly the same as the proportion of employers in service-producing industries (24.6 percent).

- When companies were asked if they used One-Stop services, 15.3 percent said they did. The use of One-Stop services increases with company size: small companies (7 percent), medium-sized companies (14.9 percent), and large companies (43.6 percent). Public administration employers are much more likely to use One-Stop services (41.5 percent) than service-producing and goods-producing employers (14.6 percent and 14.3 percent, respectively).

Job Accommodation Network

- The Job Accommodation Network (JAN) is a service that provides information on job accommodations, entrepreneurship, and related subjects. The services of JAN are familiar to 7.4 percent of companies. Large companies are much more likely to be familiar with JAN services than are small and medium-sized companies (21.6 percent compared to 6 percent and 5.9 percent, respectively). Public administration employers are more likely to be familiar with JAN (19.2 percent) than are employers in service (7.3 percent) or goods-producing industries (6.2 percent).

- Of the 7.4 percent of companies that are familiar with JAN services, 27.7 percent report using the services.

Employer Assistance and Recruiting Network

- The Employer Assistance and Recruiting Network (EARN) is a service of ODEP that assists employers in locating and recruiting qualified workers with disabilities and provides technical assistance on disability employment-related issues. Eight percent of employers are familiar with EARN services. Large companies are more likely to be familiar with EARN services than small and medium-sized companies (14.3 percent compared to 6.8 percent and 6 percent, respectively). However, there was no difference among industries types with regard to familiarity with EARN.

- Of the 8 percent of companies that are familiar with EARN services, 12.4 percent use the services.

When examining the results on challenges, concerns, and strategies, several patterns emerge. The strength of this survey is the ability to examine patterns by company size and industry. Policy initiatives can be better developed by considering these differences.

Large companies are more likely to employ, hire and actively recruit people with disabilities. This suggests that policies and information should be geared to the small and mid-sized businesses. The findings also suggest the type of information that is needed. When we asked companies that do not actively recruit people with disabilities what type of information would persuade them to recruit, information about satisfactory job performance, increases to the company's productivity, and benefits to the company's bottom line were the three most persuasive. But breaking down these results by company size revealed that small and medium companies find information about satisfactory job performance most persuasive, while large companies are most persuaded by information supported by statistics or research.

Large companies ranked inability to find qualified people with disabilities as their number one challenge. Even though large companies are more likely to be familiar with the employment services of EARN, there is room for improvement in helping companies find qualified candidates.

A high percentage of employers cited nature of the work as a concern about hiring people with disabilities, but this concern was most prevalent among employers in industries that require physically demanding work.

Not knowing how much accommodations will cost and the actual cost of accommodating disability are major concerns associated with hiring. These concerns reflect a need for education not only to increase the number of companies that recruit, but to better prepare them to make a hiring decision when considering a qualified candidate with a disability.

Health care costs, workers compensation costs and fear of litigation are more challenging for small and medium sized companies than for large companies. These challenges are especially strong among companies that do not actively recruit people with disabilities, so information geared toward allaying these fears among small and medium companies would be helpful.

For companies that employ people with disabilities, the lack of advancement potential is cited as a challenge more frequently than are attitudes of customers, co-workers or supervisors.

Small and medium companies are also challenged by the cost of workers compensation premiums and health care coverage much more than are large companies. To deal with these challenges, small and medium companies cite employer tax credits and large companies cite mentoring of employees as a successful strategy for retaining employees with disabilities. Also important to all companies is a visible top management commitment. Developing information that shows how small companies can retain their valued employees through accommodations and how mentoring works for large companies may serve to strengthen retention.

Public administration organizations tend to actively recruit and hire people with disabilities more than their private sector counterparts, which suggests a need to develop policy initiatives targeted toward the private sector.

PURPOSE OF THE EMPLOYER SURVEY

The U.S. Department of Labor, Office of Disability Employment Policy (ODEP), conducted the 2008 Survey of Employer Perspectives on the Employment of People with Disabilities. This survey emphasized current attitudes and practices of employers in 12 industry sectors, including some high growth industries as projected by the Bureau of Labor Statistics (BLS). ODEP was also interested in understanding employer perspectives by company size.

Previous surveys have documented employer response to the Americans with Disabilities Act and have identified barriers that employers experience or believe they will encounter in recruiting, hiring, retaining, and promoting workers with disabilities. For example, a 2003 telephone survey of 502 randomly selected private sector employers asked about employer views on people with disabilities in the workplace, accommodations, and economic issues (Dixon, 2003). However, there are several findings from this study that needed clarification and explanation. For example, when employers were asked what the greatest barrier to hiring people with disabilities was, 32 percent said the nature of work is such that people with disabilities cannot effectively perform it, while 22 percent answered they didn't know. Another study found that 22 percent of employers identified attitudes and stereotypes as a significant barrier to employment for people with disabilities (Bruyère, 2000). In order to increase employment opportunities for people with disabilities, it is important to know whether these beliefs are more prevalent in certain industries or vary by company size.

A literature review also revealed the following weaknesses in the methods utilized in the research about employers (Hernandez, Keys, & Balcazar, 2000; Unger, 2002):

- **Industry sectors**. Little data exist to substantiate a comparison of practices between industries.
- **High growth industries**. Little research has been conducted on companies in rapidly growing industries. There is a high likelihood that an interest in recruiting employees with disabilities may exist in these industries.
- **Company size**. Little research has compared employer perspectives on the employment of people with disabilities based on company size.

ODEP concluded that the research on employer perspectives on employing people with disabilities needed a strategic and scientifically based approach that rigorously collects and aggregates data from multiple types of employers. This survey was designed to fill a gap in knowledge about the practices and organizational challenges that employers face in recruiting, retaining, and advancing people with disabilities. There have been surveys conducted on employer attitudes, but there were no nationally representative studies on employer practices and challenges by company size and industry sector.

This survey focused on industry segments and company size to ask detailed questions about practices, challenges and strategies. The strength of this survey is its emphasis on comprehensive sampling based on industry sectors, company size, and individuals at the executive level.

This new knowledge on employer perspectives on employing people with disabilities will help ODEP formulate targeted strategies and policies for increasing employment opportunities for people with disabilities. While ODEP has conducted focus groups with high level executives, this survey provided detailed and comprehensive data on employer attitudes and practices regarding hiring, recruitment, and retention for the industries involved.

PROJECT SCOPE

The main objective of this project was to survey a nationally representative sample of senior executives representing 12 industries by company size: small (5-14 employees), medium (15-249 employees), and large companies (250 or more employees). The telephone interview was structured and contained questions to:

- Assess respondent demographics (title, number of years with company, number of years in position, number of employees supervised);
- Identify company practices in recruiting people with disabilities (number of employees with a disability, recruiting practices, information that would promote recruiting of people with disabilities);
- Address issues related to hiring and retaining employees with disabilities (perceived challenges and concerns in hiring, advancing and retaining employees with disabilities, as well as strategies to overcome these challenges);
- Assess recordkeeping on accommodations for employees with disabilities; and
- Determine familiarity with disability employment resources, such as the Job Accommodation Network (JAN), the Employer Recruiting and Assistance Network (EARN), and the One-Stop Career Centers.

SAMPLING

The target population of this survey included all employers with at least five employees in 12 industries in the United States. Firms with fewer than five employees were excluded from the target population. The three size classes were based on the total number of employees of the company: small (5-14 employees), medium (15-249 employees), and large (250 or more employees). There were a total of 36 domains of interest (three size classes within 12 industry sectors).

The survey utilized a stratified random sample design. The sample was obtained by drawing an equal probability sample of companies within each of the 36 size by industry sector strata. Larger companies were over sampled, but all companies were selected with equal probability within each stratum. Appendix A describes the sample design in detail, including the sampling frame, precision requirements, sample size, stratification, and sampling selection.

DATA COLLECTION

ODEP received OMB clearance for the survey on November 28, 2007. Westat, a leading statistical survey research organization, conducted the survey using Computer Assisted Telephone Interviewing (CATI). Special arrangements were necessary to accommodate the respondent (e.g., scheduling appointments and conducting the interview over several sessions when needed).

Pilot Test. The research team conducted a pretest of the contact procedures and the questionnaire. The contact procedures were pre-tested to insure that they allowed us to determine the correct respondent quickly. During the administration of the pre-test questionnaire, if the respondent hesitated when responding, we asked the respondent to explain the difficulty he or she was having answering the question. We timed the length of administration of the questionnaire and determined that the time did not vary significantly from the estimated administration time of 15 minutes. We also asked respondents follow-up questions, such as if they had difficulty understanding certain terms, if any of the questions did not apply to them and why, and if there was something we did not ask but should have in order to better understand the employer perspective. Once the pilot interviews were completed, we determined that the questionnaire did not need to be revised. Changes to the contact procedures were minor.

Advance Letter. An introductory letter was sent to sampled businesses. The letter was on ODEP letterhead and signed by an official at ODEP. The purpose of this letter was to introduce the study, emphasize confidentiality, explain respondent's rights, and alert the respondents that an interviewer will be calling. A toll-free number was included so that respondents could call to verify the legitimacy of the study, to ask questions or to set up an appointment for an interview. We sent all small and medium-sized businesses the advance letter prior to the interviewer's call. Large businesses were called to obtain the name of the most senior knowledgeable respondent. We then sent the advance letter to that respondent. Once the letter was sent, an interviewer called to complete the interview. If we could not speak with that respondent, we then determined the name of another knowledgeable respondent. We asked for respondents by title, using the titles cited in the questionnaire. In a large company, many of the questions on the survey were referred to Human Resources for responses. Large companies often have human resources employees who are responsible for recruiting employees with disabilities and tracking accommodations made for employees.

Interviewing began the second week of February 2008 and continued through June 2008. The advance letter and questionnaire are in Appendix B. Detailed data collection procedures are in Appendix C.

RESULTS

The statistics in this report are calculated using sample weights. In other words, the 3,797 companies in the sample represent 2,469,000 companies. A sample weight is how many companies a sample member represents. In the tables in this section, responses of "don't know" and refusals are treated as missing values. The supplementary statistical tables in Appendix D contain all estimates and corresponding standard errors, confidence intervals, and sample sizes. Estimates with coefficients of variation greater that 30 percent are indicated with daggers in the appendix tables and are not shown in the tables in this section nor interpreted in the text.

Interviews were completed with 3,797 respondents, for a response rate of 51.4 percent. Table 1 displays the number of completed interviews in each of the 36 cells.

Table 1. Number of completed interviews, by major industry sector and company size				
Major industry sector	**Number of employees**			
	5-14	**15-249**	**250 or more**	**Total**
Construction	90	98	97	285
Manufacturing	103	96	104	303
Wholesale Trade	93	111	97	301
Retail Trade	115	115	83	313
Transportation & Warehousing	98	120	105	323
Information	101	97	92	290
Finance	94	99	92	285
Professional	114	114	91	319
Education & Health	111	122	151	384
Leisure & Hospitality	113	104	103	320
Other Services	105	101	82	288
State & Local Government	125	103	158	386
Total	1,262	1,280	1,255	3,797

Employing People with Disabilities

Companies were asked, "To your knowledge, do any of your company's current employees have a physical or mental disability?" Table 2 provides the number and percentage of companies that currently employ people with disabilities. These statistics are provided for all companies and separately by company size and then by three broad industry types.[1] Among companies in the United States, 471,562 companies (19.1 percent) report employing people with disabilities.

Table 2. Number and percent of companies currently employing people with disabilities, by company size and industry		
Company size and industry	Number	Percent
All companies (5 or more employees)	471,561	19.1
Small (5–14 employees)	133,588	10.7
Medium (15–249 employees)	229,098	22.6
Large (250 or more employees)	108,875	53.1
Service-producing industries	376,905	18.9
Goods-producing industries	94,656	17.5
Public administration	19,685	42.7
Source: 2008 Survey of Employer Perspectives on the Employment of People with Disabilities, ODEP.		
Note: Based on question 10, "To your knowledge, do any of your company's current employees have a physical or mental disability?"		
All 3,797 companies were asked this question.		

With regard to company size, the larger a company, the more likely it is to employ people with disabilities. As shown in Table 2, among small companies (employing 5 to 14 people), 10.7 percent report employing people with disabilities, while 22.6 percent of mid-sized companies (employing 15 to 249 employees) and 53.1 percent of large companies (employing 250 or more employees) report employing people with disabilities. It is not surprising that companies with more employees are more likely to employ at least one employee with a disability. These companies simply have more employment opportunities and may be more likely to commit to a diverse workplace.

Employers in the public administration sector are much more likely to employ people with disabilities (42.7 percent) than employers in service-producing (18.9 percent) and goods producing industries (17.5 percent).

---

[1] These three broad industry types follow the super-sectors of the North American Industry Classification System (NAICS). Goods-producing industries include construction and manufacturing. Service-producing industries include retail trade, wholesale trade, transportation/warehousing, leisure/hospitality, education/health, information, professional, finance, and other services. Public administration is its own super-sector consisting of establishments of federal, state, and local government agencies that administer, oversee, and manage public programs and have executive, legislative, or judicial authority over other institutions within a given area.

Recruiting People with Disabilities

All companies were asked, "Does your company actively recruit job applicants who are people with disabilities?"[2] Table 3 provides the number and percent of companies that actively recruit applicants with disabilities. These statistics are provided for all companies, by company size and industry type. Table 3 shows that 326,721 companies (13.6 percent) report that they actively recruit people with disabilities. Larger companies are more likely to actively recruit people with disabilities (33.8 percent) than smaller companies (7.8 percent). In absolute numbers, there are more mid-sized companies (164,460) recruiting people with disabilities than are small (96,052) or large companies (66,209). By comparison, the distribution of companies in the United States is: 205,000 large companies, 1,014,000 mid-sized companies and 1,248,000 small companies.

Public administration organizations are more likely to actively recruit than their private sector counterparts. Among private sector companies, those in service-producing industries are more likely to actively recruit than those in goods-producing industries. Service-producing industries have the largest number of employers that actively recruit applicants with disabilities.

Table 3. Number and percent of companies that actively recruit applicants with disabilities, by company size and industry		
Company size and industry	**Number**	**Percent**
All companies (5 or more employees)	326,721	13.6
Small (5–14 employees)	96,052	7.8
Medium (15–249 employees)	164,460	16.8
Large (250 or more employees)	66,209	33.8
Service-producing industries	269,718	13.9
Goods-producing industries	39,368	9.4
Public administration	17,617	39.5
Source: 2008 Survey of Employer Perspectives on the Employment of People with Disabilities, ODEP.		
Note: Based on question 13, "Does your company actively recruit job applicants who are people with disabilities?"		
All 3,797 companies were asked this question.		

Recruiting Strategies. Companies that actively recruit people with disabilities were asked, "How do you proactively recruit job applicants who are people with disabilities?" Table 4 ranks the strategies cited by all companies; sample sizes are insufficient to generate statistics based on company size. The most frequently cited recruiting strategy is *postings at job service or workforce employment center*—23.7 percent of companies that actively recruit people with disabilities use this strategy.

---

[2] If needed, the following definition of person with a disability was read to respondents: Under the Americans with Disabilities Act, an individual with a disability is defined as a person who (1) has a physical or mental impairment that substantially limits one or more major life activities; (2) has a record of such an impairment; or (3) is regarded as having such an impairment. #

Table 4. Strategies used by companies to proactively recruit people with disabilities		
Strategy	**All companies**	
	Percent	**Rank**
Postings at job service or workforce employment center	23.7	1
Contacting college and university career centers	13.1	2
Partnerships with disability-related advocacy organizations	11.8	3
Including people w/disabilities in diversity recruitment goals	9.5	4
Postings at disability-related publications	8.8	5
Postings at disability-related websites	8.3	6
Postings or tables at disability-related job fairs	6.8	7
Postings at Department of Vocational Rehabilitation	4.0	8
Establishing summer internship and mentoring programs	NA	NA
Postings at Independent Living Centers	NA	NA
Source: 2008 Survey of Employer Perspectives on the Employment of People with Disabilities, ODEP.		
Note: Based on question 13a, "How do you proactively recruit job applicants who are people with disabilities?"		
Note: Sample sizes were insufficient to study company size.		
Statistics based on the 840 surveyed companies that actively recruit people with disabilities.		
NA indicates statistics that are not available due to insufficient sample size.		

Persuading Companies to Recruit. We asked companies that do not actively recruit people with disabilities about the type of information that would persuade them to recruit people with disabilities. Table 5 ranks the types of information cited by respondents. Information about performance, productivity, and the bottom line is considered to be the most persuasive information, while information about costs is the least persuasive. The two most cited types of information (satisfactory job performance and increases company's productivity) are consistent among small and medium-sized companies. However, large companies are more likely to be persuaded by information that is supported by statistics or research. Addressing concerns about costs is by far the least cited type of information. The relative rankings of the types of information are more consistent among small and medium-sized companies. Large companies tend to cite each type of information more often than other companies.

Table 5. Type of information that would persuade companies that do not actively recruit people with disabilities, by company size

Type of information	All companies		Small (5–14)		Medium (15–249)		Large (250 or more)	
	%	Rank	%	Rank	%	Rank	%	Rank
Satisfactory job performance, attendance and retention	68.2	1	67.4	1	68.0	1	76.4	3
Increases to your company's productivity	67.4	2	66.2	2	67.6	2	77.0	2
Benefits to your company's bottom line	65.7	3	65.0	3	65.6	3	72.3	5
Benefits other companies in your industry	63.7	4	61.5	4	64.9	4	74.2	4
Supported by statistics or research	61.0	5	58.5	5	61.8	5	77.5	1
Testimonials from human resources managers	54.6	6	52.5	6	55.0	6	69.5	6
Testimonials from senior executives	52.8	7	51.3	7	53.4	7	60.9	9
Testimonials from line managers	52.3	8	50.1	8	53.1	8	65.0	7
Benefited nationally recognized companies	46.8	9	43.7	9	48.4	9	62.7	8
Addresses concerns about costs	32.4	10	30.8	10	33.4	10	39.7	10
Source: 2008 Survey of Employer Perspectives on the Employment of People with Disabilities, ODEP.								
Note: Based on question 14, "Would any of the following types of information persuade you to recruit people with a disability?"								
Statistics based on the 2,857 companies that do not actively recruit people with disabilities. Also excluded from the calculations are companies that said they already have the information.								

Hiring People with Disabilities

Table 6 provides the number and percentage of companies that hired a person with disabilities in the past 12 months. These statistics are provided for all companies and separately by company size and then by three broad industry types. Table 6 shows that 215,344 companies (8.7 percent) report having hired people with disabilities in the past 12 months. This is substantially lower than the 19.1 percent of companies that reported employing people with disabilities. As with employing people with disabilities, large companies are more likely to report having hired a person with disabilities (32.6 percent) compared to medium-sized companies at 8.0 percent.

Table 6. Number and percent of companies that hired a person with disabilities in the past 12 months, by company size and industry

Company size and industry	Number	Percent
All companies (5 or more employees)	215,344	8.7
Small (5–14 employees)	67,459	5.4
Medium (15–249 employees)	81,173	8.0
Large (250 or more employees)	66,714	32.6
Service-producing industries	178,417	9.0
Goods-producing industries	27,959	6.5
Public administration	8,960	19.7
Source: 2008 Survey of Employer Perspectives on the Employment of People with Disabilities, ODEP.		
Note: Based on question 12, "In the past 12 months has your company hired any people with disabilities?"		
All 3,797 companies were asked this question.		

Hiring Challenges. All companies were asked, "I am now going to describe several factors in hiring people with disabilities that we often hear from employers. How much of a challenge are the following factors to your company in *hiring* people with disabilities? I would like you to say whether it is a major challenge, somewhat of a challenge or not a challenge."

Table 7 provides the percentage of companies that cited a particular factor as a major challenge or somewhat of a challenge. The percentages and rankings are provided for each factor for all companies and by company size.

The nature of the work being such that it cannot be effectively performed by a person with a disability is cited as a challenge by 72.6 percent of all companies. Attitudes of co-workers or supervisors are least frequently cited as a challenge, especially for small and medium size companies. When looking across company size, the rankings suggest that health care costs, workers compensation costs and fear of litigation are more challenging for small and medium sized companies than for large companies.

Also note that not knowing how much accommodations will cost is considered more of a hiring challenge than the actual cost of accommodation, which suggests that aversion to risk may be a challenge that needs to be addressed in the cost of accommodation literature.

Table 7. Percent of companies citing challenges in hiring people with disabilities, by company size								
Challenge	All companies		Small (5–14)		Medium (15–249)		Large (250 or more)	
	%	Rank	%	Rank	%	Rank	%	Rank
Nature of the work	72.6	1	73.7	1	72.4	1	67.1	2
Not knowing how much accommodation will cost	63.7	2	63.9	2	63.5	3	63.4	3
Cannot find qualified people with disabilities	63.6	3	61.7	4	65.1	2	68.0	1
Actual cost of accommodating disability	61.6	4	63.0	3	60.9	4	57.1	4
Concern about cost of workers compensation premiums	47.4	5	54.8	5	43.3	5	22.8	12
Concern about the cost of health care coverage	46.2	6	52.6	6	42.0	6	27.8	10
Fear of litigation	40.6	7	45.0	7	38.0	8	26.6	11
Lack of knowledge or information	39.7	8	39.4	8	39.2	7	44.3	5
Attitudes of customers	34.3	9	35.8	9	31.7	9	38.3	6
Discomfort or unfamiliarity	32.2	10	34.5	10	29.9	10	29.5	9
Attitudes of co-workers	29.1	11	28.1	11	29.7	11	32.0	8
Attitudes of supervisors	20.3	12	17.8	12	21.1	12	32.1	7
Source: 2008 Survey of Employer Perspectives on the Employment of People with Disabilities, ODEP.								
Note: Based on question 15, "I am now going to describe several factors in hiring people with disabilities that we often hear from employers. How much of a challenge are the following factors to your company in hiring people with disabilities? I would like you to say whether it is a major challenge, somewhat of a challenge or not a challenge."								
All 3,797 companies were asked this question.								

Because such a large percentage of respondents cited the nature of the work as a hiring challenge, we examined this response by industry. Table 8 presents the percentage of companies reporting the nature of the work as a challenge to hiring people with disabilities, across industries. Companies in the construction, manufacturing (goods-producing industries) and retail trade industries are most likely to cite the nature of the work, while companies in the financial services, professional services, and information services industries are the least likely to cite the nature of the work. In fact, in the follow-up question, companies cited the difficult physical demands as the reason why a person with a disability could not effectively perform the jobs within their companies.

Table 8. Percent of companies citing the nature of the work as a challenge to hiring people with disabilities, by industry	
Industry	**Percent**
All companies	72.6
Construction	88.8
Manufacturing	84.9
Retail trade	83.7
Transportation and warehousing	78.7
Leisure and hospitality	77.0
Wholesale trade	76.1
Public administration	74.6
Education and health	68.1
Other services	63.0
Information services	59.2
Professional services	58.8
Finance services	56.2
Source: 2008 Survey of Employer Perspectives on the Employment of People with Disabilities, ODEP.	
Note: Based on question 15, "I am now going to describe several factors in hiring people with disabilities that we often hear from employers. How much of a challenge are the following factors to your company in hiring people with disabilities? I would like you to say whether it is a major challenge, somewhat of a challenge or not a challenge."	
All 3,797 companies were asked this question.	

Since all companies were asked about hiring challenges, we split the respondents into two groups: those that actively recruit people with disabilities and those that do not. As shown in Table 9, the rankings of the factors are remarkably similar for the two groups. Table 9 also shows the percentage difference between companies that recruit and companies that do not recruit. Overall, companies that do not recruit people with disabilities are more likely to report a particular factor to be a challenge—with the notable exception of lack of knowledge or information. The biggest differences between companies that recruit and those that do not recruit are in the challenges related to workers compensation costs, health insurance costs, fear of litigation, actual cost of accommodations, and attitudes of co-workers.

Table 9. Percent of companies citing challenges in hiring people with disabilities, by whether the company actively recruits people with disabilities

Challenge	All companies		Actively Recruits				Percent Difference
			Yes		No		
	%	Rank	%.	Rank	%	Rank	
Nature of the work	72.6	1	61.5	1	74.4	1	-17.4
Not knowing how much accommodation will cost	63.7	2	52.4	3	65.8	2	-20.4
Cannot find qualified people with disabilities	63.6	3	58.6	2	64.6	3	-9.3
Actual cost of accommodating disability	61.6	4	45.3	4	64.3	4	-29.6
Concern about cost of workers compensation premiums	47.4	5	30.7	8	50.7	5	-39.5
Concern about the cost of health care coverage	46.2	6	31.6	6	48.8	6	-35.2
Fear of litigation	40.6	7	30.1	9	42.6	7	-29.3
Lack of knowledge or information	39.7	8	42.5	5	39.2	8	8.4
Attitudes of customers	34.3	9	31.6	7	35.1	9	-9.8
Discomfort or unfamiliarity	32.2	10	27.0	10	32.9	10	-18.0
Attitudes of co-workers	29.1	11	21.5	11	30.4	11	-29.2
Attitudes of supervisors	20.3	12	16.8	12	20.9	12	-19.4

Source: 2008 Survey of Employer Perspectives on the Employment of People with Disabilities, ODEP.

Note: Based on question 15, "I am now going to describe several factors in hiring people with disabilities that we often hear from employers. How much of a challenge are the following factors to your company in hiring people with disabilities? I would like you to say whether it is a major challenge, somewhat of a challenge or not a challenge."

All 3,797 companies were asked this question.

Hiring Concerns. All companies were asked, "Some employers have concerns about hiring people with disabilities. Here are some of the concerns we often hear from employers. For each, please let me know how much of a concern it is for your company."

Table 10 shows the percent of companies that cite a particular concern as a major concern or somewhat of a concern. The percentages and rankings are provided for each concern for all companies and by company size. As shown in Table 10, the cost of employing people with disabilities and the belief that workers with disabilities lack the skills and experience necessary are the most often cited concerns for small and mid-sized companies, while it is the supervisor's uncertainty about how to take disciplinary action that is cited most often for large companies. In contrast, supervisors not comfortable with managing people with disabilities is the least cited by small and medium sized companies, but still accounts for about a third of these companies. That people with disabilities may not be as safe and productive as other workers is the least cited concern by large companies.

Table 10. Percent of companies citing concerns about hiring people with disabilities, by company size								
Concern	**All companies**		**Small (5–14)**		**Medium (15–249)**		**Large (250 or more)**	
	%	Rank	%	Rank	%	Rank	%	Rank
It costs more to employ workers with disabilities	58.1	1	64.0	1	54.4	1	39.7	5
Workers with disabilities lack the skills and experience to do our jobs	49.4	2	52.1	2	47.6	2	41.5	4
People with disabilities may not be as safe and productive as other workers	45.7	3	49.9	3	42.7	4	35.0	6
Supervisors are not sure how to take disciplinary action	44.3	4	44.4	4	43.6	3	47.6	1
Supervisors are not sure how to evaluate	40.7	5	39.8	5	41.3	5	43.1	3
Supervisors are not comfortable with managing	30.8	6	28.7	6	30.5	6	44.9	2
Source: 2008 Survey of Employer Perspectives on the Employment of People with Disabilities, ODEP.								
Based on question 19, "Some employers have concerns about hiring people with disabilities. Here are some of the concerns we often hear from employers. For each, please let me know how much of a concern it is for your company." The following responses were available: a major concern somewhat of a concern or not a concern.								
All 3,797 companies were asked this question.								

Table 11 splits the respondents into two groups: those that actively recruit people with disabilities and those that do not. As shown in Table 11, the rankings of the concerns differ. The biggest differences between companies that recruit and those that do not recruit are in the concerns related to safety and productivity, skills and experience, and cost, with companies that do not recruit citing these concerns more frequently than companies that recruit people with disabilities.

Table 11. Percent of companies citing concerns about hiring people with disabilities, by whether the company actively recruits people with disabilities							
Concern	**All companies**		**Actively Recruits**				**Percent Difference**
			Yes		**No**		
	%	Rank	%	Rank	%	Rank	
It costs more to employ workers with disabilities	58.1	1	44.1	1	60.7	1	-27.4
Workers with disabilities lack the skills and experience to do our jobs	49.4	2	36.3	4	51.4	2	-29.4
People with disabilities may not be as safe and productive as other workers	45.7	3	30.5	5	48.4	3	-37.0
Supervisors are not sure how to take disciplinary action	44.3	4	42.5	2	44.8	4	-5.0
Supervisors are not sure how to evaluate	40.7	5	39.8	3	40.7	5	-2.2
Supervisors are not comfortable with managing	30.8	6	25.6	6	31.7	6	-19.0
Source: 2008 Survey of Employer Perspectives on the Employment of People with Disabilities, ODEP.							
Based on question 19, "Some employers have concerns about hiring people with disabilities. Here are some of the concerns we often hear from employers. For each, please let me know how much of a concern it is for your company."							
All 3,797 companies were asked this question.							

Helpful Hiring Strategies. All companies were asked about strategies that would be helpful in hiring people with disabilities. Table 12 ranks these strategies. Regardless of company size, the top five strategies to facilitate hiring are very similar across company size: employer tax credits, disability awareness training, visible top management commitment, mentoring, and assistive technology. The relative rankings of the other strategies vary by company size, with tax credits most important to small and medium companies and visible top management commitment most important to large companies. Small companies are also more likely to cite flexible work schedules as a strategy to facilitate hiring. And regardless of company size, a centralized accommodations fund and reassignment are the least cited strategies. The larger the company size, the more likely a given strategy is cited.

Table 12. Percent of companies citing hiring strategies that would be helpful in hiring people with disabilities, by company size								
Strategy	**All companies**		**Small (5–14)**		**Medium (15–249)**		**Large (250 or more)**	
	%	Rank	%	Rank	%	Rank	%	Rank
Employer tax credits and incentives	69.2	1	66.8	1	70.5	1	77.1	5
Disability awareness training	64.3	2	59.1	5	66.9	2	82.8	3
Visible top management commitment	64.2	3	59.4	4	65.8	3	84.9	1
Mentoring	63.4	4	60.7	2	62.3	4	84.3	2
Assistive technology	61.1	5	59.1	5	59.7	6	80.3	4
Using a specialized recruiting source	60.8	6	57.3	7	61.8	5	76.6	6
Flexible work schedule	60.0	7	59.7	3	58.1	7	71.8	12
Training existing staff	57.9	8	54.7	8	58.0	8	76.1	7
On-site consultation or technical assistance	57.1	9	54.5	9	57.0	9	73.1	9
Disability targeted internship program	55.4	10	53.0	10	54.4	11	74.3	8
Short-term on the job assistance with job coach	54.3	11	50.5	11	55.2	10	72.4	10
Developing a targeted recruitment program	50.7	12	47.3	12	50.5	12	72.2	11
Centralized accommodations fund	47.1	13	43.3	13	48.4	13	64.1	13
Reassignment	40.1	14	37.8	14	40.1	14	54.5	14
Source: 2008 Survey of Employer Perspectives on the Employment of People with Disabilities, ODEP.								
Note: Based on question 20, "I will read you a few strategies that some companies have used when hiring people with disabilities. For each, please tell me if these strategies would be helpful in reducing barriers to hiring people with disabilities into your company." Yes/no responses were available.								
All 3,797 companies were asked this question.								

Table 13 splits the respondents into two groups: those that actively recruit people with disabilities and those that do not. As shown in Table 13, the rankings of the three most cited strategies (employer tax credits and incentives, disability awareness training, and visible top management commitment) and of the two least cited strategies (centralized accommodations fund and reassignment) are the same regardless of whether a company actively recruits. Table 13 also shows that for each of the strategies, companies that do not recruit people with disabilities are less likely to report a strategy to be helpful than companies that recruit people with disabilities. The biggest difference between those that recruit and those that do not recruit is in developing a targeted recruitment program, with companies that actively recruit more likely to cite this as helpful in reducing barriers to hiring.

Table 13. Percent of companies citing hiring strategies that would be helpful in hiring people with disabilities, by whether the company actively recruits people with disabilities

Strategy	All companies		Actively recruits				Percent difference
			Yes		No		
	%	Rank	%	Rank	%	Rank	
Employer tax credits and incentives	69.2	1	82.8	1	67.0	1	23.7
Disability awareness training	64.3	2	80.8	3	61.2	3	32.1
Visible top management commitment	64.2	3	81.2	2	61.5	2	32.1
Mentoring	63.4	4	78.8	5	60.9	4	29.5
Assistive technology	61.1	5	79.2	4	58.1	5	36.5
Using a specialized recruiting source	60.8	6	78.0	6	57.7	7	35.2
Flexible work schedule	60.0	7	73.7	8	57.7	6	27.7
Training existing staff	57.9	8	73.5	9	55.5	8	32.5
On-site consultation or technical assistance	57.1	9	71.6	12	54.9	9	30.4
Disability targeted internship program	55.4	10	71.7	11	52.8	10	35.9
Short-term on the job assistance with job coach	54.3	11	72.3	10	51.3	11	40.9
Developing a targeted recruitment program	50.7	12	73.8	7	46.9	12	57.5
Centralized accommodations fund	47.1	13	61.9	13	44.8	13	38.3
Reassignment	40.1	14	58.4	14	37.1	14	57.2

Source: 2008 Survey of Employer Perspectives on the Employment of People with Disabilities, ODEP.

Note: Based on question 20, "I will read you a few strategies that some companies have used when hiring people with disabilities. For each, please tell me if these strategies would be helpful in reducing barriers to hiring people with disabilities into your company." Yes/no responses were available.

All 3,797 companies were asked this question.

Advancing People with Disabilities

Advancement Challenges. Companies that currently employ people with disabilities were asked about factors in advancing a person with a disability. Table 14 provides the percent of companies that cited each factor as a major challenge or somewhat of a challenge. The actual cost of accommodation and lack of advancement potential are the top two cited challenges to advancing employees with disabilities, regardless of company size, far surpassing attitudes of customers, co-workers or supervisors.

Table 14. Percent of companies that employ people with disabilities citing challenges to advancing employees with disabilities, by company size

Challenge	All companies		Small (5–14)		Medium (15–249)		Large (250 or more)	
	Pct.	Rank	Pct.	Rank	Pct.	Rank	Pct.	Rank
Actual cost of accommodating disability	43.9	1	51.3	2	42.1	1	38.5	1
Lack of advancement potential	41.4	2	52.4	1	39.3	2	32.6	2
Attitudes of customers	25.3	3	29.4	3	24.4	3	22.0	5
Attitudes of co-workers	21.4	4	20.3	4	21.4	4	23.1	4
Attitudes of supervisors	19.4	5	16.4	5	17.7	5	26.7	3

Source: 2008 Survey of Employer Perspectives on the Employment of People with Disabilities, ODEP.

Note: Based on question 17, "In your opinion, how much of a challenge are the following factors to your company in advancing a person with a disability?" The following responses were available: a major challenge, somewhat of a challenge or not a challenge.

Statistics based on the 1,148 companies that employ people with disabilities.

Helpful Advancement Strategies. Companies that currently employ people with disabilities were also asked about strategies that would be helpful in advancing people with disabilities. Table 15 provides the percentage of companies that cited a particular strategy and the rank of each strategy. In contrast to hiring strategies shown in Table 12, where employer tax credits and incentives were the least cited strategy regardless of company size, employer tax credits and incentives are the most frequently cited strategy for advancing employees with disabilities for small and mid-sized companies. The difference from the results in Table 12 may be due to the fact that all companies were asked about hiring strategies, while Table 15 is based on companies that employ people with disabilities. A visible commitment from top management is important to advancing people with disabilities, regardless of company size. The least cited strategy— reassignment—is common across company size.

Table 15. Percent of companies that employ people with disabilities citing advancement strategies, by company size

Strategy	All companies		Small (5–14)		Medium (15–249)		Large (250 or more)	
	%	Rank	%	Rank	%	Rank	%	Rank
Employer tax credits and incentives	77.2	1	82.6	1	75.3	1	74.7	6
Visible top management commitment	75.2	2	70.3	3	73.5	2	84.8	1
Mentoring	74.0	3	71.3	2	70.6	4	84.3	2
Disability awareness training	71.6	4	62.1	7	71.9	3	82.7	3
Assistive technology	68.7	5	65.5	5	66.0	7	78.5	4
Flexible work schedule	68.1	6	68.7	4	67.4	5	68.7	9
Training existing staff	67.1	7	59.5	9	66.9	6	76.5	5
On-site consultation or technical assistance	65.5	8	58.3	10	66.0	7	73.4	7
Short-term on the job assistance with job coach	63.7	9	60.2	8	62.1	9	71.1	8
Disability targeted internship program	60.1	10	64.1	6	54.8	10	66.7	11
Centralized accommodations fund	54.7	11	53.7	11	49.1	11	67.7	10
Reassignment	49.7	12	52.9	12	47.0	12	51.5	12

Source: 2008 Survey of Employer Perspectives on the Employment of People with Disabilities, ODEP.

Note: Based on question 21, "For each of the following, please tell me if these strategies would be helpful in advancing people with disabilities within your company." Yes/no responses were available.

Statistics based on the 1,148 companies that employ people with disabilities.

Retaining People with Disabilities

Retention Challenges. Companies that currently employ people with disabilities were asked, "In your opinion, how much of a challenge are the following factors to your company in retaining a person with a disability?" Table 16 provides the percent of companies that cite a particular factor as a major challenge or somewhat of a challenge. Finding ways to return employees to work after the onset of a disability is the number one challenge to medium and large companies. For small companies, it is the actual cost of accommodation, followed by finding ways to return employees to work. Costs of health-care and workers compensation are less of a challenge to retention for larger companies. Again, attitudes are the least frequently cited challenge by small and medium-sized companies.

Table 16. Percent of companies that employ people with disabilities citing challenges to retaining employees with disabilities, by company size

Challenge	All companies		Small (5–14)		Medium (15–249)		Large (250 or more)	
	%	Rank	%	Rank	%	Rank	%	Rank
Finding a way to return employees to work	51.3	1	53.3	2	49.1	1	53.6	1
Lack of advancement potential	45.9	2	53.2	3	45.2	2	38.5	2
Actual cost of accommodating disability	42.3	3	53.9	1	40.1	3	32.8	3
Concern about the cost of workers compensation premiums	35.4	4	51.7	4	33.7	4	19.7	7
Concern about the cost of health care coverage	32.9	5	50.4	5	29.7	5	18.7	8
Attitudes of customers	22.4	6	23.5	6	20.8	7	24.3	4
Attitudes of co-workers	21.2	7	19.3	7	21.8	6	22.1	6
Attitudes of supervisors	18.9	8	14.7	8	19.1	8	23.4	5

Source: 2008 Survey of Employer Perspectives on the Employment of People with Disabilities, ODEP.

Note: Based on question 18, "In your opinion, how much of a challenge are the following factors to your company in retaining a person with a disability?" The following responses were available: a major challenge, somewhat of a challenge or not a challenge.

Statistics based on the 1,148 companies that employ people with disabilities.

Helpful Retention Strategies. Companies that currently employ people with disabilities were asked about strategies that would be helpful in retaining people with disabilities. Table 17 shows how the strategies rank by company size. A visible commitment from top management is important to retaining people with disabilities, regardless of company size. Small and mid-sized companies are more likely to cite employer tax credits and incentives as a retention strategy than large companies. Large companies most often cite mentoring as the top strategy for retention. In fact, except for employer tax credits or incentives, large companies cite each strategy more frequently than small or medium companies, perhaps because they are more likely to hire and actively recruit people with disabilities than their smaller counterparts. Regardless of company size, the two least cited strategies are a centralized accommodations fund and reassignment.

Table 17. Percent of companies that employ people with disabilities citing retention strategies, by company size

Strategy	All companies		Small (5–14)		Medium (15–249)		Large (250 or more)	
	%	Rank	%	Rank	%	Rank	%	Rank
Visible top management commitment	75.2	1	73.1	2	72.2	2	83.9	2
Employer tax credits and incentives	75.2	1	81.1	1	73.1	1	72.3	6
Mentoring	72.0	3	69.7	3	67.0	4	85.2	1
Flexible work schedule	69.4	4	68.5	4	69.2	3	71.1	8
Assistive technology	68.8	5	66.8	5	64.8	6	79.7	4
Disability awareness training	68.3	6	63.3	7	66.7	5	77.9	5
On-site consultation or technical assistance	67.0	7	62.6	8	63.4	7	80.0	3
Training existing staff	65.5	8	64.4	6	63.1	8	71.7	7
Short-term on the job assistance with job coach	62.1	9	59.0	9	60.4	9	69.5	9
Disability targeted internship program	57.8	10	57.3	10	53.8	10	66.7	10
Centralized accommodations fund	54.3	11	55.0	11	48.0	11	66.7	10
Reassignment	50.5	12	51.5	12	47.8	12	55.2	12

Source: 2008 Survey of Employer Perspectives on the Employment of People with Disabilities, ODEP.

Note: Based on question 22, "For each of the following, please tell me if these strategies would be helpful in retaining people with disabilities within your company." Yes/no responses were available.

Statistics based on the 1,148 companies that employ people with disabilities.

Collecting Accommodations Data

Workplace accommodations play an important role in the productivity of people with disabilities. Companies that employ people with disabilities were asked about the purposes for keeping data on the accommodations for employees with disabilities. Table 18 provides the percentage of the companies that keep data for a particular reason and how those reasons rank by company size. Regardless of company size, the top two reasons are regulatory reporting requirements (36.4 percent) and disability claim coordination (32.2 percent), while the least cited is tracking accommodation costs (13.3 percent). Large companies cited each reason more frequently than other companies.

Table 18. Percent of companies that cited reasons for collecting data on accommodations, by company size

Reason for collecting data on accommodations	All companies		Small (5–14)		Medium (15–249)		Large (250 or more)	
	%	Rank	%	Rank	%	Rank	%	Rank
Regulatory reporting requirements	36.4	1	21.9	1	37.4	1	52.0	1
Disability claim coordination	32.2	2	20.6	2	31.4	2	48.1	2
Future accommodations in similar situations	24.8	3	19.5	3	21.3	4	38.5	4
Dispute resolution/settlement	24.0	4	16.9	4	21.5	3	38.8	3
Tracking accommodation costs	13.3	5	12.2	5	12.2	5	16.9	5

Source: 2008 Survey of Employer Perspectives on the Employment of People with Disabilities, ODEP.

Note: Based on question 23, "Does your company keep data on the accommodations it makes for employees with disabilities for any of the following purposes?"

Statistics based on the 1,148 companies that employ people with disabilities.

Knowledge of One-Stop Career Centers

One-Stop Career Centers are operated by state and local agencies and are designed to provide a full range of assistance to job seekers and employers in one location. Established under the Workforce Investment Act, the centers offer training referrals, career counseling, job listings, and other employment-related services. All companies were asked, "Are you aware that your local One-Stop Center offers services to businesses?" Table 19 shows that 25 percent of employers are aware of local One-Stop Centers. Large companies (42.6 percent) and employers in public administration (38.1 percent) are more likely to know of local One-Stop Centers. Within the private sector, the proportion of employers in goods-producing industries aware of One-Stop services is the roughly the same as the proportion of employers in service-producing industries.

When companies were asked if they used One-Stop services, 15.3 percent said they did. The use of One-Stop services increases with company size: small companies (7 percent), medium-sized companies (14.9 percent), and large companies (43.6 percent). Public administration employers are much more likely to use One-Stop services (41.5 percent) than service-producing and goods-producing employers (14.6 percent and 14.3 percent, respectively).

Table 19. Percent of companies aware of the services of the One-Stop Career Centers and percent of those companies that used One-Stop services, by company size and industry type		
Company size and industry type	**Percent aware of One-Stop Career Centers**	**Percent that used services among those aware**
All companies (5 or more employees)	25.0	15.3
Small (5–14 employees)	21.6	7.0
Medium (15–249 employees)	25.6	14.9
Large (250 or more employees)	42.6	43.6
Service-producing industries	24.6	14.6
Goods-producing industries	25.5	14.3
Public administration	38.1	41.5
Source: 2008 Survey of Employer Perspectives on the Employment of People with Disabilities, ODEP.		
Note: Based on question 26a, "One-Stop Career Centers are publicly-operated by State and local agencies and are designed to provide a full range of assistance to job seekers and employers in one location. Established under the Workforce Investment Act, the centers offer training referrals, career counseling, job listings, and similar employment-related services. Are you aware that your local One-Stop Center offers services to businesses?" and question 26b: "In the past 12 months, has your company used any of those business services from the One-Stop Center?"		
All 3,797 companies were asked question 26a.		

Respondents were also asked which services they used. However, the sample of respondents that used One-Stop services was too small—not all strata are represented—therefore standard errors could not be estimated.

Knowledge of the Job Accommodation Network

The Job Accommodation Network (JAN) is a service provided by ODEP. Its mission is to facilitate the employment and retention of workers with disabilities by providing information on job accommodations, entrepreneurship, and related subjects. All companies were asked, "Are you familiar with the services of the Job Accommodation Network?" Table 20 shows that 7.4 percent of employers are familiar with JAN services. Large companies are much more likely to be familiar with JAN services than small and medium-sized companies (21.6 percent compared to 6 percent and 5.9 percent, respectively). Public administration employers are more likely to be familiar with JAN (19.2 percent) than are employers in service (7.3 percent) or goods-producing industries (6.2 percent).

Of the companies that are familiar with JAN services, 27.7 percent report using the services.

Table 20. Percent of companies familiar with the services of the Job Accommodation Network (JAN) and percentage of those companies that used JAN services, by company size and industry type		
Company size and industry type	Percent familiar	Percent that used services among those familiar
All companies (5 or more employees)	7.4	27.7
Small (5–14 employees)	6.0	NA
Medium (15–249 employees)	5.9	NA
Large (250 or more employees)	21.6	NA
In service-producing industries	7.3	NA
In goods-producing industries	6.2	NA
In public administration	19.2	NA
Source: 2008 Survey of Employer Perspectives on the Employment of People with Disabilities, ODEP.		
Note: Based on question 24, "Are you familiar with the services of the Job Accommodation Network?" and question 24a, "Have you used the services of the Job Accommodation Network?"		
All 3,797 companies were asked question 24.		
NA indicates that estimates are not available due to small sample size.		

Knowledge of the Employer Assistance and Recruiting Network

The Employer Assistance and Recruiting Network (EARN) is a service provided by ODEP. It is a national toll-free telephone and electronic information referral service which became available to the public in March 2001. It assists employers in locating and recruiting qualified workers with disabilities and provides technical assistance on general disability employment-related issues. All companies were asked, "Are you familiar with the services of the [EARN]?" Table 21 shows that 8 percent of employers are familiar with EARN services. As with JAN services, large companies are more likely to be familiar with EARN services than are small and medium-sized companies (14.3 percent compared to 6.8 percent and 6 percent, respectively). However, there was no difference among the three types of industries with regard to familiarity with EARN.

Companies that indicated familiarity with EARN services were asked if they used these services. Table 21 shows that 12.4 percent of these companies use EARN services.

Table 21. Percent of companies familiar with the services of the Employer Assistance and Recruiting Network (EARN) and percent of those companies that used EARN services, by company size and industry type		
Company size and industry type	Percent familiar	Percent that used services among those familiar
All companies (5 or more employees)	8.0	12.4
Small (5–14 employees)	6.8	NA
Medium (15–249 employees)	8.0	NA
Large (250 or more employees)	14.3	NA
In service-producing industries	8.1	NA
In goods-producing industries	7.6	NA
In public administration	8.6	NA
Source: 2008 Survey of Employer Perspectives on the Employment of People with Disabilities, ODEP.		
Note: Based on question 25, "Are you familiar with the services of the Employer Assistance and Recruiting Network (EARN)?" and question 25a, "Have you used the services of the EARN?"		
All 3,797 companies were asked question 25.		
NA indicates that estimates are not available due to small sample size.		

Limitations of the data

When delving deeper into specific issues, it will be important to consider the number of companies that can address these issues. For instance, when looking at recruiting strategies, the sample was limited to the 840 respondents that actively recruit people with disabilities, restricting the ability to analyze this issue by company size and industry. However, this finding is a useful indicator that more needs to be done to encourage employers to actively recruit people with disabilities.

When studying disability issues, it is important to consider cultural and experiential differences. For instance, there is concern that the prevalence of disability in some states is too high or too low because of systematic differences in the way people perceive disability. Vignette approaches have been used successfully to obtain quasi-baseline information about respondent perception. In this approach, the interviewer reads a vignette about an individual, and then respondent is asked if the person in the vignette has a disability. After several vignettes, the respondent is asked if he or she has a disability. A similar approach could be used to solicit information about an employer's perspective regarding the nature of disability and the types of jobs employers believe that people with a disability can and cannot do.

Conclusions

When examining the results on challenges, concerns, and strategies, several patterns emerge. The strength of this survey is the ability to examine patterns by company size and industry. Policy initiatives can be better developed by considering these differences.

Large companies are more likely to employ, hire and actively recruit people with disabilities. This suggests that policies and information should be geared to the small and mid-sized businesses. The findings also suggest the type of information that is needed. When we asked companies that do not actively recruit people with disabilities what type of information would persuade them to recruit, information about satisfactory job performance, increases to the company's productivity, and benefits to the company's bottom line were the three most persuasive. But breaking down these results by company size revealed that small and medium companies find information about satisfactory job performance most persuasive, while large companies are most persuaded by information supported by statistics or research.

Large companies ranked inability to find qualified people with disabilities as their number one challenge. Even though large companies are more likely to be familiar with the employment services of EARN, there is room for improvement in helping companies find qualified candidates.

A high percentage of employers cited nature of the work as a concern about hiring people with disabilities, but this concern was most prevalent among employers in industries that require physically demanding work. When probed, some companies cited sales work as being difficult for a person with a disability to perform because of the travel involved. This may reflect a lack of knowledge about accommodations available and these employers may benefit from information on how travel is not necessarily a barrier for people with disabilities.

Not knowing how much accommodations will cost and the actual cost of accommodating disability are major concerns associated with hiring. At the same time, not knowing how much accommodations will cost is considered more of a hiring challenge than the actual cost of accommodation, which suggests that aversion to risk needs to be addressed in the literature on the cost of accommodations. These concerns reflect a need for education not only to increase the number of companies that recruit, but to better prepare them to make a hiring decision when considering a qualified candidate with a disability.

Health care costs, workers compensation costs and fear of litigation are more challenging for small and medium sized companies than for large companies. These challenges are especially strong among companies that do not actively recruit people with disabilities, so information geared toward allaying these fears among small and medium companies would be helpful.

For companies that employ people with disabilities, the lack of advancement potential is cited as a challenge more frequently than are attitudes of customers, co-workers or supervisors. Not surprisingly, lack of advancement potential was more of challenge for small companies than for medium and large companies.

Companies are challenged by finding ways to return employees to work after the onset of a disability, and for small firms, the cost of accommodating disability was the major challenge in retaining employees with disabilities. These findings show that return to work can present special challenges even for companies that already employ people with disabilities, and for small companies that must bear the cost of accommodations. Small and medium companies are also challenged by the cost of workers compensation premiums and health care coverage much more than are large companies. To deal with these retention challenges, small and medium companies cite employer tax credits and large companies cite mentoring of employees as a successful strategy for retaining employees with disabilities. Also important to all companies is a visible top management commitment. Developing information that shows how small companies can retain their valued employees through accommodations and how mentoring works for large companies may serve to strengthen retention.

Public administration organizations tend to actively recruit and hire people with disabilities more than their private sector counterparts, which suggests a need to develop policy initiatives targeted toward the private sector.

REFERENCES

Bruyère, S. M. (2000). *Disability employment policies and practices in private and federal sector organizations.* Ithaca, NY: Cornell University, School of Industrial and Labor Relations Extension Division, Program on Employment and Disability.

Dixon, K.A. (2003). *Restricted access: A survey of employers about people with disabilities and lowering barriers to work.* Rutgers, NJ: The John J. Heldrich Center for Workforce Development.

Hernandez, B., Keys, C., & Balcazar, F. (2000). Employer attitudes toward workers with disabilities and their ADA employment rights: A literature review. *Journal of Rehabilitation, 66,* 4-16.

Unger, D.D. (2002). Employers' attitudes toward people with disabilities in the workforce: Myths or realities. *Focus on Autism and Other Developmental Disabilities, 17*(1), 2-10.

Appendix A: Sample Design

This appendix describes the sample design. It includes a description of the sampling frame, precision requirements and sample size, stratification, and sample selection.

Sampling Frame

The sampling frame for the survey was the Duns Market Identifiers (DMI) register maintained by Dun & Bradstreet (D&B). DMI is a file produced by D&B, Inc., contains basic company data, executive names and titles, mailing and location addresses, corporate linkages, D-U-N-S numbers, employment and sales data on over 10 million U.S. business establishment locations, including public, private, and government organizations. DMI is the single comprehensive publicly available database to provide coverage of business establishments. An alternative comprehensive database is BusinessUSA, however it does not provide corporate linkages and only a small number of records can be accessed at a time and thus it is not convenient for drawing random samples. Other alternative databases are generally restricted to certain sectors.

DMI's coverage of the target population is relatively complete. A Westat study, conducted in eight states, found that its coverage of establishments is high[1]. The study claims that the coverage of establishments, based on the eight states, appears to be near 98 or 99 percent. However, coverage of new establishments can be much lower. The study in eight states found that about one-half of new establishments are included in the list within the first year. The coverage of smaller establishments can also be relatively lower.

The sampling frame records contained the following fields from DMI: a D-U-N-S number; North American Industry Classification System (NAICS) code and Standard Industrial Classification (SIC code); FIPS State code; SMSA code; number of employees at the location; total number of employees for the entire organization; status indicator, i.e., single location, headquarters, or branch; a subsidiary indicator; D-U-N-S numbers of the domestic topmost firm, headquarters, and parent (if a subsidiary); a hierarchy code to identify its location within the corporate structure; and DIAS code.

Employer policies and practices on the employment of people with disabilities may vary among large firms. Some may be highly centralized; others may have separate policies in branches. DMI provided the option of choosing alternative organizational levels. The DMI list included both headquarters and branch level records. DMI defines a headquarters as a business establishment that has branches or divisions reporting to it, and is financially responsible for those branches or divisions. We included only the headquarters record for those companies with multiple branches. Therefore, the sampling units were the single location (a business establishment with no branches or subsidiaries reporting to it) companies and the headquarters of the companies that have multiple branches. The headquarters record provided the total number of employees for the company, including the employees in the branches. Another corporate family linkage relationship provided by DMI is the subsidiary to parent linkage. A subsidiary is a corporation with more than 50 percent of its capital stock is owned by another corporation and will have a different legal business name from its parent company. The subsidiaries and parent companies were included as separate sampling units.

---

[1] Marker, David A. and Sherm Edwards (1997). " Quality of the DMI File as a Business Sample Frame." Proceedings of the Section on Survey Research Methods, American Statistical Association, 1997, pp. 21-30.

Precision Requirements and Sample Size Determination

The domains of the population of interest for the survey were based on company size classes within the major industry sectors. The 12 industry sectors and their definitions in terms of 2002 NAICS codes are shown in Table A.1.

The size classes were small, medium, and large. The size classes were based on the total number of employees of the company. A uniform set of size class boundaries was used for all industry sectors, e.g., small (5-14 employees), medium (15-249 employees), and large companies (250 or more employees). There were a total of 36 (three size classes within 12 industry sectors) domains of interest.

Table A1. Definition of Major Industry Sectors by 2002 NAICS Codes	
Industry Sector	**2002 NAICS**
Construction	23: Construction
Manufacturing	31-33: Manufacturing
Wholesale Trade	42: Wholesale Trade
Retail Trade	44-45: Retail Trade
Transportation and Warehousing	48: Transportation
	492: Couriers & Messengers
	493: Warehousing & Storage
Information	51: Information
Financial Activities	52: Finance and Insurance
	53: Real Estate and Rental and Leasing
Professional & Business Services	54: Professional, Scientific, and Technical Services
	55: Management of Companies and Enterprises
	56: Administrative and Support and Waste Management and Remediation Services
Education & Health Services	61: Education Services
	62: Health Care and Social Assistance
Leisure & Hospitality	71: Arts, Entertainment, and Recreation
	72: Accommodation and Food Services
Other Services	81: Other Services
Public Administration	92: Public Administration

Table A.2 shows the number of company records in the sampling frame by major industry sector and company employee size classes. Single location companies and headquarters of companies with multiple branches were used in the sampling frame. That is, a company with a headquarters and multiple branches in different locations was included as a single unit. The number of employees for the headquarters refers to the total number of employees in the company, including the employees in the branches. The number of employees includes full-time and part-time employees as well as the owners/proprietors.

28

Table A2. Number of Companies by Major Industry Sector and Company Employee Size Sampling Strata

Industry Sector	Number of Employees			
	5-14	15-249	250 or more	Total
Construction	203,555	102,087	2,634	308,276
Manufacturing	124,616	119,963	12,676	257,255
Wholesale Trade	128,176	69,984	3,371	201,531
Retail Trade	243,026	102,809	3,298	349,133
Transportation & Warehousing	45,064	32,364	1,920	79,348
Information	37,732	35,259	2,364	75,355
Financial Activities	155,783	86,982	5,875	248,640
Professional & Business Services	322,603	145,739	8,429	476,771
Education & Health Services	263,654	197,577	15,657	476,888
Leisure & Hospitality	164,051	325,885	4,368	494,304
Other Services	222,110	67,055	1,688	290,853
Public Administration	10,796	39,922	4,478	55,196
Total	1,921,166	1,325,626	66,758	3,313,550

Note: The companies with an unknown employee size are included in the 15-249 size category.

About 1.5 percent of the total number of companies had an unknown employee size.

The population parameters of interest are mainly in the form of proportions. These include within each company size class and industry sector, the proportion of companies with employees that have disability, the proportion of companies that hired any person with disabilities within the past 12 months, the proportion of companies that proactively recruit job applicants who are people with disabilities, etc. For example, the estimate of the proportion of companies with employees having disability in size class k within industry sector h, $\hat{p}_{hk}$ will be obtained as:

$$\hat{p}_{hk} = \frac{\sum_{i \in S_{hk}} w_{hki} y_{hki}}{\sum_{i \in S_{hk}} w_{hki}}$$

where,

S_{hk} is the set of responding companies in company size class k within industry sector h;

w_{hki} is the nonresponse adjusted sampling weight attached to responding company i in company size class k within industry sector h (see the weighting section below for the derivation of the sampling weights);

y_{hki} is the indicator of the presence of an employee with disability in company i in company size class k within industry sector h.

The sample size in each size class within the major industry sector should be large enough to provide a sufficient number of completed interviews to obtain estimates with a reasonable precision. We decided to select a sample to yield 100 completed interviews in each of the 36 size class by industry sector strata. Therefore, in total, we targeted to obtain 3,600 completed interviews. The maximum percent error for estimates of percentages obtained from a simple random sample yielding 100 completed interviews should not exceed 10 percent, 95 percent of the time. The percent error is the largest for a 50 percent proportion and decreases as proportion moves further away from the 50 percent / 50 percent split. For example, for an 80 percent / 20 percent split, the error is 8 percent. Thus, 100 completed interviews in each of the size by industry strata should provide an adequate precision level for estimates of percentages.

There is also interest in comparing the proportions across company size classes and industry sectors. The sample sizes should be large enough to provide more than 80 percent power to detect reasonable differences in proportions. The power of a test is the probability of rejecting the null hypothesis of no difference between two proportions, when the null hypothesis is false and the alternative hypothesis is true. If the power of the test is inadequate, when the null hypothesis of no difference is not rejected, we can not conclude with a reasonable confidence that there is no difference between the proportions because this may be due to the fact that the sample size is too small to detect the difference. A power of 80 percent is generally considered as adequate. Given, a certain power level, larger sample sizes are needed to detect smaller differences. A sample size of 100 can detect, with more than 80 percent power, differences of only about 20 percent or larger. Thus, with the planned sample size of 100 in each stratum, in comparing proportions between company size classes within a given industry sector or between industries within a given size class, differences of only about 20 percent or larger can be detected with adequate power. Smaller differences can be detected with adequate power if comparisons are made across industry sectors as aggregated across the size classes or between the company size classes as aggregated across the industry sectors.

The overall target response rate for the survey was 40 percent. Therefore, to obtain 3,600 completed interviews, we needed to contact 9,000 eligible companies. We assumed varying eligibility rates across size classes. We assumed 20 percent of companies selected from the small size stratum, 5 and 2 percents of companies selected from the medium and large size strata, respectively, will be identified with less than 5 employees in the interview and thus will be ineligible for the survey. In addition, we assumed 20 percent of companies selected from small size strata and 10 percent from medium and large strata will be found as out-of-business. We also increased the sample size by 20 percent to allow for a reserve sample. Note that it was not possible to identify and exclude the federal government agencies from the D&B's sampling frame. This has to be done after the sample selected by screening in the beginning of the interview. We increased the sample size of the public administration sector, by about 10 percent to allow for screening and excluding the federal government agencies from the survey. Thus, the initial total sample size was determined to be 14,654 company records.

Stratification and Sample Selection

The sampling strata were formed by three (small, medium, and large) size classes within each major industry sector. The small, medium, and large size strata were defined as: 5-14 employees, 15-249 employees, and 250 or more employees. The companies were selected with equal probability within each size by industry sector stratum. The sample selection was independent across these sampling strata.

After selecting the initial sample, the sampled records in each of the 36 employee size and industry sector strata were partitioned into approximately equal sized random groups. These random groups were released in waves to the data collection center to conduct interviews, as needed. In total, we released 9,118 company records for interview. Note that the number of random groups released varied across industry/size sampling strata to achieve the goal of obtaining close to 100 completed interviews in each reported industry/size stratum. Table A.3 shows the number of company records released in each industry/size sampling stratum.

Table A3. Number of Companies Released for Interview by Major Industry Sector and Company Employee Size Sampling Strata				
Industry Sector	**Number of Employees**			
	5-14	**15-249**	**250 or more**	Total
Construction	299	202	234	735
Manufacturing	269	203	214	686
Wholesale Trade	296	221	236	753
Retail Trade	269	203	254	726
Transportation & Warehousing	354	202	275	831
Information	324	243	331	898
Financial Activities	352	282	255	889
Professional & Business Services	271	200	258	729
Education & Health Services	271	203	179	653
Leisure & Hospitality	272	260	234	766
Other Services	271	203	256	730
Public Administration	303	224	195	722
Total	3,551	2,646	2,921	9,118

Sampling Weights

The sampling weight is attached to every company record with a completed interview (1) to account for differential probabilities of selection across the industry/size sampling strata and (2) to reduce the potential bias resulting from nonresponse. The sampling weights are necessary for unbiased estimation of the population characteristics of interest in this survey.

The first step in derivation of the sampling weights was to derive a base weight, which is the reciprocal of the probability of selection of the company. Then, the base weights were adjusted for nonresponse in order to reduce potential biases resulting from not obtaining an interview with every company in the sample. These adjustments were made by redistributing the weights of nonresponding companies to responding companies with similar propensities for nonresponse. A predictive model for response propensity was developed to identify subgroups of population with differential response rates within industry/size sampling strata. These subgroups were then used as nonresponse adjustment cells and a separate weight adjustment was applied in each cell. The potential predictors that can be used in this modeling effort have to be known for both respondents and nonrespondents. These include major industry sector, company employee size classes, Census region, MSA/non-MSA status, and single location company or headquarters identifier for the company.

If response propensity is independent of survey estimates within nonresponse adjustment cells, then nonresponse-adjusted weights yield unbiased estimates. There are several alternative methods of forming nonresponse adjustment cells to achieve this result. We used Chi-Square Automatic Interaction Detector (CHAID) software (SPSS, 1993[2]) to guide us in forming the cells. CHAID partitions data into homogenous subsets with respect to response propensity. To accomplish this, it first merges values of the individual predictors, which are statistically homogeneous with respect to the response propensity and maintains all other heterogeneous values. It then selects the most significant predictor (with the smallest p-value) as the best predictor of response propensity and thus forms the first branch in the decision tree. It continues applying the same process within the subgroups (nodes) defined by the "best" predictor chosen in the preceding step. This process continues until no significant predictor is found or a specified (about 20) minimum node size is reached. The procedure is stepwise and creates a hierarchical tree-like structure.

All sample companies were classified into five major survey response categories based on the outcome of the survey. These five categories were:

- respondent – interview completed;
- nonrespondents, identified as inscope (in business) but eligibility (based on the interview) could not be determined (company name and being in business were verified but was not able to conduct the interview);
- identified as inscope (in business) but determined to be ineligible in the interview;
- inscope (in business) status could not be verified (mainly nonlocatable cases);
- out-of-scope (company is no longer in business).

See Table 8.1 for a detailed breakdown of these major response categories by survey disposition codes and the number of sampled cases. Note that we refer to cases that were identified as being no longer in business as out-of-scope. A number of companies although they were in business (which we refer as

---

[2] SPSS (1993), SPSS for Windows: CHAID, Release 6.0, User's Guide, Jay Magidson/SPSS Inc., 1993.

inscope), later were identified as ineligible during the interview, for such reasons as, with less than 5 employees, a federal government agency, etc.

We developed separate models for the nonresponding companies with unknown inscope status (nonlocatables) and for the nonresponding inscope companies. After forming two separate sets of adjustment cells, we first adjusted the weights to compensate for those nonresponding companies with unknown inscope status. This weight adjustment factor was computed within each adjustment cell, as the ratio of the weighted (by the base weight) total number of sampled companies to the weighted number of companies, whose inscope status could be determined. In the second step, we adjusted the weights to compensate for nonresponding inscope companies. This nonresponse adjustment factor was computed as the ratio of the weighted (after adjusting for nonlocatables) number of all inscope companies (including those identified as ineligible in the interview) to the weighted number of companies, whose eligibility could be determined (the companies with a completed interview plus those that were identified as ineligible in the interview) within each nonresponse adjustment cell. Next, we discuss each weight adjustment in detail and present the formulae.

Adjusting the Weights to Compensate for Nonresponding Cases with Unknown Inscope Status (nonlocatables)

First, the weights were adjusted to compensate for nonresponding cases with unknown inscope status (nonlocatables). The adjustment factor for the adjustment class c (λ_c) was computed as:

$$\lambda_c = \frac{\sum_{i \in S_{1c}} W_{ci}^B + \sum_{i \in S_{2c}} W_{ci}^B + \sum_{i \in S_{3c}} W_{ci}^B + \sum_{i \in S_{4c}} W_{ci}^B + \sum_{i \in S_{5c}} W_{ci}^B}{\sum_{i \in S_{1c}} W_{ci}^B + \sum_{i \in S_{2c}} W_{ci}^B + \sum_{i \in S_{3c}} W_{ci}^B + \sum_{i \in S_{5c}} W_{ci}^B}$$

where,

S_{1c} is the set of companies with a completed interview in adjustment class c,

S_{2c} is the set of nonresponding inscope companies in adjustment class c,

S_{3c} is the set of companies that were identified as ineligible in the interview in adjustment class c,

S_{4c} is the set of sampled cases with undetermined inscope status (nonlocatables) in adjustment class c,

S_{5c} is the set of out-of-scope (no longer in business) sample cases in adjustment class c,

W_{ci}^B is the base weight for company record i in adjustment class c.

Then, the weight adjusted for the nonresponding cases with unknown inscope status (nonlocatables) for sampled record i in adjustment class c, (W_{ci}^U), was computed as:

$$W_{ci}^U = W_{ci}^B \times \lambda_c$$

33

Adjusting the Weights for Nonresponding Inscope Companies

After forming the nonresponse adjustment cells, the weights were adjusted to compensate for the nonresponding inscope companies. This nonresponse adjustment factor for cell α, δ_α was computed as:

$$\delta_\alpha = \frac{\sum_{i \in S_{1\alpha}} W_{\alpha i}^U + \sum_{i \in S_{2\alpha}} W_{\alpha i}^U + \sum_{i \in S_{3\alpha}} W_{\alpha i}^U}{\sum_{i \in S_{1\alpha}} W_{\alpha i}^U + \sum_{i \in S_{3\alpha}} W_{\alpha i}^U}$$

where,

$S_{1\alpha}$ is the set of companies with a completed interview in adjustment class α,

$S_{2\alpha}$ is the set of nonresponding inscope companies in adjustment class α,

$S_{3\alpha}$ is the set of companies that were found to be ineligible during the interview in adjustment class α,

$W_{\alpha i}^U$ is the weight adjusted for unknown inscope cases for provider i in adjustment class α.

Then, the final nonresponse adjusted weight was computed by multiplying the weight that was adjusted for the nonresponding cases with unknown inscope status, with the nonresponse adjustment factor. The final nonresponse adjusted sample weight for company i in nonresponse adjustment class α, $W_{\alpha i}^F$, was computed as follows:

$$W_{\alpha i}^F = W_{\alpha i}^U \times \delta_\alpha$$

Response Rate

The survey achieved a final survey response rate of 51.4 percent. Table A.4 shows the major response categories defined by disposition codes and the number of sampled cases.

Table A4. Major response categories, survey disposition codes, and the number of sampled cases

Major Response Categories and Disposition Codes	Number of Sampled Cases
Total Sample	**9,118**
1. Respondent - Completed Interview	**3,797**
C1: Complete	3,797
2. Nonrespondent - Inscope - Eligibility unknown	**3,169**
RB: Final refusal	799
RM: Maximum call refusal	423
LM: Maximum number attempts to administer survey to respondent with problem communicating in English	53
LP: Final inability to administer survey in English	3
MC: Maximum contact in English	1,835
MR: Maximum number calls on a refusal case	33
NO: No way found to reach a contact without a name or extension due to IVR systems or company policy	22
NP: Not available in field period	1
3. Inscope - Ineligible in interview	**817**
I2: fewer than 5 employees	714
I3: Federal government agency	48
I4: Ineligible industry, e.g., agricultural, utility	3
I5: Company does no hiring (company has volunteers or elected personnel only)	41
I6: All hiring done outside of U.S.	4
I7: All hiring outsourced, e.g. by unions, outside employment agencies	7
4. Nonrespondent - Unknown Inscope status	**1,207**
MP: Maximum number phone numbers tried & establishment unfound	2
MT: Maximum number call attempts made across more than 1 phone number	11
NL: Nonlocatable	1,194
5. Out-of-Scope	**128**
OC: Not in business	127
OD: Duplicate	1

In Table 8.1, the first major response category includes respondents, who completed the interview. The second category includes inscope nonrespondents, who are identified as being in business but was unable to conduct the interview. The third category includes inscope companies that were identified as ineligible in the interview. The fourth category includes those cases whose inscope status could not be determined (mostly nonlocatables). The out-of-scope category includes mostly the cases that were no longer in business.

The unweighted response rate is calculated as:

$$R = 100 \times \frac{S_1}{S_1 + bS_2 + abS_4}$$

where,

S_1 is the number of completed interviews,

S_2 is the number of inscope nonrespondents whose eligibility could not be determined,

S_4 is the number of nonrespondents whose inscope status could not be determined,

b is the estimated proportion of sample inscope cases of unknown eligibility that are eligible,

a is the estimated proportion of sample cases of unknown inscope status that are inscope,

b is estimated as:

$$b = \frac{S_1}{S_1 + S_3}$$

a is estimated as:

$$a = \frac{S_1 + S_2 + S_3}{S_1 + S_2 + S_3 + S_5}$$

where

S_3 is the number of inscope sample cases that are determined to ineligible in the interview,
S_5 is the number of sample cases that are identified as out-of-scope.

The weighted response rate for this survey is calculated as 54.4 percent.

Appendix B: Advance Letter and Questionnaire

Dear _____

The Office of Disability Employment Policy (ODEP) at the U.S. Department of Labor provides policy analysis and technical assistance to increase employment opportunities for people with disabilities and to assist employers. ODEP is interested in learning how employers in various industries successfully recruit and retain employees with disabilities. Gathering this information from senior executives will promote effective partnerships between ODEP and employers in developing innovative practices and strategies that will improve the employment of people with disabilities. Additional information about ODEP is available at www.dol.gov/odep.

Your company has been randomly selected to participate in the *Survey of Employer Perspectives on the Employment of People with Disabilities*. Westat is conducting the interviews for the Department of Labor. Within the next few weeks, someone from Westat will call you to complete a short interview. Your cooperation is essential to the success of this effort to identify successful practices and share them with other employers. Individually identifiable data will be accessible only to authorized project staff at Westat. Individual responses are analyzed only in combination with other responses collected nationwide. The responses will not be linked with your company or with your name.

Privacy: Responses to this data collection will be used only for statistical purposes. The reports prepared for this study will summarize findings across the sample and will not associate responses with a specific firm or individual. We will not provide information that identifies you or your firm to anyone outside the study team, except as required by law.

As required by the Paperwork Reduction Act, ODEP received approval from the Office of Management and Budget (OMB) (approval number 1230-0005). The approval covers sampling businesses and conducting executive interviews to better inform ODEP's policies.

You may call Westat at 1-888-280-4573 if you have any questions about the study, or to set an appointment for an interview. Please call me if you have any questions about this survey at 202-693-4923. Thank you for your assistance in this project.

Sincerely,

Richard Horne
Supervisory Research Analyst, Research and Evaluation Team

Survey of Employer Perspectives on the Employment of People with Disabilities

IF LARGE COMPANY, FIRST ASK:

SC1.   Hello, may I please have the name of your company president? [IF NEEDED: I am calling from Westat, a survey research firm in Rockville, MD. We need to send some information about a survey we are conducting for the U.S. Department of Labor.]

Name _____   _____

SC2.   And would we address a letter to him/her at [ADDRESS ON FILE}?

Yes	1	
No	2 °	**[GO TO SC3]**
Refused	-7	
Don't know	-8 →	

SC3.   May I please have the correct address?

_____   _____

Number   Street

_____

Suite/Office number

_____   _____   _____

City   State   Zip code

Thank-you very much.

PACKAGE WILL BE MAILED. WHEN INTERVIEWER CALLS BACK, INTERVIEW WILL START AT SC4.

SC4.   Hello. May I please speak with {NAME OF EXECUTIVE TO WHOM THE LETTER WAS MAILED}?

[My name is {INTERVIEWER'S NAME} and I am calling on behalf of the U. S. Department of Labor. {EXECUTIVE'S NAME} recently received a letter about a study of people with disabilities.]

Available/coming to the phone	1 →	**[GO TO SC6]**
Not available	2	
At another telephone number	3	
No such person/no longer here/new respondent needed.......4 →		**[GO TO SC5]**
Telephone company recording...	5	
Answering machine/voice mail...	AM	
Retry dialing	RT	
Go to result..	GT	

SC5.   I'd like to speak with someone else who makes decisions on hiring at the overall company level such as your company President or Human Resources Manager. Would you please connect me to such a person?

[alternate titles:
President/owner
Vice-president, finance
Vice-president, human resources
Vice president
Director
Assistant director
Manager
Assistant manager
Supervisor]

Speaking/coming to the phone..1 → **[GO TO SC6]**
Collect name of best respondent 2
Don't know best respondent; callback 3
Go to result... GT

SC6.   Hello, my name is [INTERVIEWER NAME], and I am calling from Westat, a research firm in Rockville, MD. We are conducting a survey for the U.S. Department of Labor. We recently sent a letter introducing the study. This is a brief survey of business executives in high growth industries to see what opportunities might be available in these industries for people with disabilities. The survey will take about 20 minutes.

This survey is for research purposes only and is not part of an investigation or audit by the Department of Labor. Your cooperation is voluntary. Your responses will not be linked with your company or with your name. First, I would like to ask about your business.

[IF NEEDED: You can skip any question you do not want to answer, and you can stop at anytime.]

I. Demographic Information.

1. We show that your business is mostly in the {BUSINESS TYPE} industry group. Is that correct?

Yes	1	
No	2	[go to 1a]
Refused	-7	°
Don't know	-8	→

1a. Mostly what type of business is it?

Construction	1
Wholesale trade	2
Retail trade	3
Transportation and warehousing	4
Information	5
Financial activities	6
Professional and business services	7
Education and health services	8
Leisure and hospitality	9
Equipment and machinery repairing	10
Promoting or administering religious activities	11
Grantmaking	12
Advocacy	13
Drycleaning and laundry services	14
Personal care services	15
Death care services	16
Pet care services	17
Photofinishing services	18
Temporary parking services	19
Dating services	20
State and local government	21
Manufacturing	22
Other	91
(specify) _____	
Refused	-7
Don't know	-8

2. We show you have {NUMBER OF EMPLOYEES}. Is that correct?
[IF NEEDED: Please count all employees, not just full time employees.]

Yes 1
No .... 2 → [GO TO 2a]
Refused .... -7 °
Don't know .... -8 →

2a. Including your corporate headquarters, subsidiaries, and branches, how many employees does your business have? Would you say…
[IF NEEDED: Please count all employees, not just full time employees.]

Fewer than 5, ... 1 → [GO TO THANKB]
5 to 14, ... 2
15 to 249, or 3
250 or more? 4
Refused .... -7
Don't know .... -8

THANKB: Thank-you, but we are only interested in companies with 5 or more employees.

3. How many employees do you have at your location?

     [IF NEEDED: Please count all employees, not just full time employees.]

     _____ Number of employees at location

     Refused .... -7
     Don't know .... -8

4. We show your business headquarters is in {STATE}. Is that correct?

     Yes 1
     No .... 2 ↑ **[GO TO 4a]**
     Refused .... -7 →
     Don't know .... -8 →

     4a. In what state or U.S. territory is your business <u>headquartered</u>?
          [IF NEEDED: We want to know where your U.S. headquarters is located.]

Alabama	1	Montana	29
Alaska	2	Nebraska...	30
American Samoa.....................	3	Nevada	31
Arkansas	4	New Hampshire.................................	32
Arizona	5	New Jersey	33
California	6	New Mexico	34
Colorado	7	New York	35
Connecticut............................	8	North Carolina..................................	36
Delaware	9	North Dakota.....................................	37
District of Columbia		Northern Mariana	
(Washington, DC)............................	10	Islands	38
Florida...................................	11	Ohio...	39
Georgia	12	Oklahoma	40
Guam.....................................	13	Oregon..	41
Hawaii	14	Pennsylvania	42
Idaho	15	Puerto Rico..	43
Illinois...................................	16	Rhode Island	44
Indiana	17	South Carolina...................................	45
Iowa	18	South Dakota.....................................	46
Kansas	19	Tennessee	47
Kentucky................................	20	Texas	48
Louisiana...............................	21	U.S. Virgin Islands............................	49
Maine	22	Utah...	50
Maryland................................	23	Vermont	51
Massachusetts	24	Virginia	52
Michigan................................	25	Washington	53
Minnesota	26	West Virginia	54
Mississippi	27	Wisconsin..	55
Missouri	28	Wyoming...	56

          Refused .... -7
          Don't know .... -8

5.   We show <u>your</u> location is in {STATE}. Is that correct?

Yes	1		
No	2	→	[GO TO 5a]
Refused	-7	°	
Don't know	-8	→	

5a.   In what state or U.S. territory are you located?

Alabama	1		Montana	29
Alaska	2		Nebraska........................	30
American Samoa............	3		Nevada	31
Arkansas	4		New Hampshire..............	32
Arizona	5		New Jersey	33
California	6		New Mexico...................	34
Colorado	7		New York	35
Connecticut	8		North Carolina...............	36
Delaware	9		North Dakota.................	37
District Of Columbia			Northern Mariana	
(Washington, DC)..........	10		Islands	38
Florida..........................	11		Ohio..............................	39
Georgia	12		Oklahoma......................	40
Guam............................	13		Oregon..........................	41
Hawaii..........................	14		Pennsylvania	42
Idaho............................	15		Puerto Rico	43
Illinois	16		Rhode Island	44
Indiana	17		South Carolina...............	45
Iowa	18		South Dakota.................	46
Kansas..........................	19		Tennessee	47
Kentucky......................	20		Texas	48
Louisiana......................	21		U.S. Virgin Islands...........	49
Maine	22		Utah..............................	50
Maryland......................	23		Vermont	51
Massachusetts	24		Virginia	52
Michigan	25		Washington	53
Minnesota	26		West Virginia	54
Mississippi	27		Wisconsin......................	55
Missouri	28		Wyoming.......................	56

Refused	-7
Don't know	-8

6. What is your job title?

    President/Owner... 1
    Vice-President, Finance 2
    Vice-President, Human Resources.. 3
    Vice President 4
    (Specify) _____
    Director 5
    Assistant Director 6
    Manager 7
    Assistant Manager.. 8
    Supervisor 9
    Other 91
    (Specify) _____
    Refused .... -7
    Don't Know .... -8

7. About how many years have you been working for {COMPANY NAME}?

    _____ Number

    Refused .... -7
    Don't know .... -8

8. About how many years have you been the {RESPONSE FROM 6}?

    _____ Number

    Refused .... -7
    Don't know .... -8

9. How many employees do you supervise?

    [IF NEEDED: Please count all employees, not just full time employees.]

    _____ Number

    Refused .... -7
    Don't know .... -8

10. To your knowledge, do any of your company's current employees have a physical or mental disability?

> [IF NEEDED: *Under the Americans with Disabilities Act, an individual with a disability is defined as a person who (1) has a physical or mental impairment that substantially limits one or more major life activities; (2) has a record of such an impairment; or (3) is regarded as having such an impairment.*

Yes, ...	1 →	[GO TO 11]
I'm not sure, or..	2 ↑	
No, not to my knowledge?	3 °	[GO TO 12]
Refused	-7 .	
Don't know	-8 →	

11. Do you happen to know how many employees in your company have a disability?

_____ Number

We don't track that information..	DT
Not sure how many	NS
Refused	-7
Don't know	-8

12. In the past 12 months has your company hired any people with disabilities?

Yes, ...	1
No, not to my knowledge, or I'm not sure?	2
Refused	-7
Don't know	-8

13. Does your company actively recruit job applicants who are people with disabilities?

Yes	1 →	[GO TO 13a]
No	2 ↑	
Refused	-7 °	[GO TO 14]
Don't Know	-8 →	

13a. How do you proactively recruit job applicants who are people with disabilities?

[CODE ALL THAT APPLY. Probe: Any other ways?]

Including people with disabilities in diversity recruitment goals.................	1
Creating partnerships with disability- related advocacy organizations	2
Contacting career centers at colleges and universities when vacancies arise	3
Posting job announcements in disability-related publications	4
Posting job announcements on disability-related websites	5
Posting job announcements and/or hosting a table at disability-related job fairs	6
Establishing summer internship and mentoring programs targeted at youth with disabilities	7
Posting jobs with centers for independent Living (CILS)...........................	8
Posting jobs with the department of Vocational rehabilitation	9
Posting jobs with the job service or workforce employment center (if needed: unemployment Offices)...	10
Other ways	91
(specify) _____	
Refused	-7
Don't know	-8

IF 13=1, YES, GO TO Q15.

14. Would any of the following types of information persuade you to recruit people with a disability? What about...

Response categories: **Yes, No , Already Have This Information/ Already Know This, Refused, Don't Know**
a. Information that addresses your concerns about costs?
b. Information showing how hiring people with disabilities has benefited other companies in your industry?
c. Information showing how hiring people with disabilities has benefited nationally recognized companies, for example a Fortune 500 company?
d. Information showing how hiring people with disabilities can benefit your company's bottom line?
e. Information showing how hiring people with disabilities can increase your company's productivity?
f. Information that is supported by statistics or research?
g. Information on satisfactory job performance, attendance, and retention of people with disabilities?
h. Testimonial information of senior executives attesting to the success for their companies?
i. Testimonial information of human resources managers attesting to the success for their companies?
j. Testimonial information of line managers attesting to the success for their companies?
91. Anything else? (SPECIFY_____)

15. I am now going to describe several factors in hiring people with disabilities that we often hear from employers. How much of a challenge are the following factors to your company in <u>hiring</u> people with disabilities? I would like you to say whether it is a major challenge, somewhat of a challenge or not a challenge.

   a. Discomfort or unfamiliarity regarding hiring people with disabilities? Would you say this is a major challenge, somewhat of a challenge or not a challenge?

   b. Lack of knowledge or information about people with disabilities

   c. Attitudes of co-workers

   d. Attitudes of supervisors

   e. Attitudes of customers

   f. Not knowing how much accommodation will cost

   g. Actual cost of accommodating disability

   h. Concern about the cost of health care coverage

   i. Concern about the cost of workers compensation premiums

   j. Fear of litigation

   k. You cannot find qualified people with disabilities

   l. The nature of the work is such that it cannot be effectively performed by people with disabilities

   91. Anything else?...
        (SPECIFY_____)

IF L =1, YES, GO TO 16.

---

16. Can you please describe the nature of the job or jobs in your company which would pose a challenge to a person with a disability?

   _____

   _____

PROGRAMMER NOTE: IF 10=1, YES, ASK 17 AND 18. ELSE, SKIP TO 19.

47

17. In your opinion, how much of a challenge are the following factors to your company in <u>advancing</u> a person with a disability? How about…

    a. Attitudes of co-workers? Would you say this is a major challenge, somewhat of a challenge or not a challenge?

    b. Attitudes of supervisors
    c. Attitudes of customers
    d. Actual cost of accommodating disability
    e. Lack of advancement potential
    91 Anything else? (SPECIFY_____)

18. In your opinion, how much of a challenge are the following factors to your company in <u>retaining</u> a person with a disability?

    a. Lack of opportunity for advancement [IF NEEDED: Would you say this is a major challenge, somewhat of a challenge or not a challenge?]
    b. Attitudes of co-workers
    c. Attitudes of supervisors
    d. Attitudes of customers
    e. Actual cost of accommodating a disability
    f. Concern about the cost of health care coverage
    g. Concern about the cost of workers compensation premiums
    h. Finding a way to return employees to work who have been on disability leave or workers compensation
    91 Anything else? (Specify_____)

19. Some employers have concerns about hiring people with disabilities. Here are some of the concerns we often hear from employers. For each, please let me know how much of a concern it is for your company.

    a. Supervisors are not comfortable managing people with disabilities. [IF NEEDED: Would you say this is a major concern, somewhat of a concern or not a concern?]
    b. Supervisors are not sure how to evaluate a person with a disability.

    c. Supervisors are not sure how to take disciplinary action for a person with a disability.

    d. Workers with disabilities lack the skills and experience to do our jobs
    e. People with disabilities may not be as safe and productive as other workers.
    f. It costs more to employ workers with disabilities than those without disabilities due to accommodations, additional management time, or healthcare and insurance costs
    91 Anything else? (SPEC IFY_____)

20. I will read you a few strategies that some companies have used when hiring people with disabilities. For each, please tell me if these strategies would be helpful in reducing barriers to <u>hiring</u> people with disabilities into your company.

        a.   Using a recruiting source that specializes in placing people with disabilities
        b.   Developing a targeted recruitment program for people with disabilities
        c.   Short-term on the job assistance with an outside job coach?
        d.   Training existing staff
        e.   On-site consultation or technical assistance
        f.   Mentoring
        g.   Visible top management commitment
        h.   Centralized accommodations fund [IF NEEDED: A company-wide fund to provide accommodations for people with disabilities]..........
        i.   Disability awareness training
        j.   Disability targeted internship program
        k.   Assistive technology
        l.   Flexible work schedule
        m. Employer tax credits and incentives
        n.   Reassignment
        91. Anything else
             (SPECIFY_____)

IF 10=1, YES, ASK 21, 22, AND 23. ELSE, SKIP TO 24.

---

21. For each of the following, please tell me if these strategies would be helpful in <u>advancing</u> people with disabilities within your company.

        a.   Short-term on the job assistance with an outside job coach
        b.   Training existing staff
        c.   On-site consultation or technical assistance
        d.   Mentoring
        e.   Visible top management commitment
        f.   Centralized accommodations fund [IF NEEDED: A company-wide fund to provide accommodations for people with disabilities].
        g.   Disability awareness training
        h.   Disability targeted internship program
        i.   Assistive technology
        j.   Flexible work schedule
        k.   Reassignment
        l.   Employer tax credits and incentives
        91. Anything else? (SPECIFY_____)

22. For each of the following, please tell me if these strategies would be helpful in <u>retaining</u> people with disabilities within your company.

    a. Short-term on the job assistance with an outside job coach
    b. Training existing staff
    c. On-site consultation or technical assistance
    d. Mentoring
    e. Visible top management commitment
    f. Centralized accommodations fund [IF NEEDED: A company-wide fund to provide accommodations for people with disabilities]
    g. Disability awareness training
    h. Disability targeted internship program
    i. Assistive technology
    j. Flexible work schedule
    k. Reassignment
    l. Employer tax credits and incentives
    91. Anything else? (SPECIFY_____)

23. Does your company keep data on the accommodations it makes for employees with disabilities for any of the following purposes?

    a. Future accommodations in similar situations
    b. Tracking accommodation costs
    c. Dispute resolution/settlement
    d. Regulatory reporting requirements
    e. Disability claim coordination
    f. Anything else?
       SPECIFY_____)
    g. Do not keep data on accommodations

24. Are you familiar with the services of the Job Accommodation Network? [IF NEEDED: The Job Accommodation network, also known as JAN, "facilitates the employment and retention of workers with disabilities by providing employers, employment providers, people with disabilities, their family members and other interested parties with information on job accommodations." Their website is http://www.jan.wvu.edu/]

    Yes .... 1 → [GO TO 24a]
    No .... 2 ↑ [GO TO 25]
    Refused .... -7 ° [GO TO 25]
    Don't know .... -8 →

    24a. Have you used the services of the Job Accommodation Network?

        Yes 1
        No 2
        Refused .... -7
        Don't know .... -8

25. Are you familiar with the services of the Employer Assistance and Recruiting Network (EARN)? [IF NEEDED: EARN is a free service that connects employers looking for quality employees with skilled job candidates. Their website is http://www.earnworks.com/]

Yes	1	→ [GO TO 25a]
No	2	[GO TO 26]
Refused	-7 °	[GO TO 26]
Don't know	-8	→

    25a.   Have you used the services of EARN?

Yes	1
No	2
Refused	-7
Don't know	-8

26. One-Stop Career Centers are publicly-operated by State and local agencies and are designed to provide a full range of assistance to job seekers and employers in one location. Established under the Workforce Investment Act, the centers offer training referrals, career counseling, job listings, and similar employment-related services.

    26a. Are you aware that your local One-Stop Center offers services to businesses?

A. Yes..	1	→ [GO TO 26b]
B. No	2	[GO TO 27]
C. Never heard of a One-Stop..............	3	[GO TO 27]
D. D/K...	4	[GO TO 27]
E. Refused.......................................	5	[GO TO 27]

    26b.   In the past 12 months, has your company used any of those business services from the One-Stop Center?

A. Yes..	1	→ [GO TO 26c]
B. No...	2	[GO TO 27]
C. D/K...	3	[GO TO 27]
D. Refused.......................................	4	[GO TO 27]

26c.   I will now ask you a series of questions about business services that your company may have used with the One-Stop Center. In the past 12 months, has the One-Stop center provided your company with …..

A.   recruitment, job referral, and candidate screening?
B.   Job task analysis to formally identify knowledge skills and abilities for specific jobs?
C.   Outplacement services for employees?
D.   Analysis of local business trends?
E.   Analysis of the local labor pool?
F.   Disability Program Navigator Staff
G.   Assistance in recruiting qualified workers?
H.   Assistance to customize training plans for new hires?
I.   An offer to train current employees?
J.   Literacy, ESL or basic skills training for current or prospective employees?
K.   Services on to help your company with specific HR issues, such as high turnover?
L.   Services on how to create employment opportunities, such as recruitment, retention, and promotion, for individuals with disabilities?
M.   Other services? _____
N.   Don't know

[If needed for option F: Disability Program Navigators (DPN). In 2002, the Department of Labor's Employment (DOL) and Training Administration (ETA) and the Social Security Administration (SSA) established a new position, ***the Disability Program Navigator (DPN),*** located within DOL's One-Stop Career Center. The ***DPN, or Navigator,*** guides One-Stop Career Center staff in helping people with disabilities to access and navigate the complex provisions of various programs that impact on their ability to gain and retain employment. In addition, the DPNs: develop linkages and collaborate on an ongoing basis with employers to facilitate the employment of people with disabilities; develop partnerships to achieve integrated services, system change, and expand the capacity of the One-Stop Career Centers to serve customers with disabilities; conduct outreach to agencies/organizations that serve people with disabilities; serve as resources on SSA's work incentives; serve as resources on the federal, state, and local programs that impact on the ability of people with disabilities to enter into and remain in the workforce; and facilitate the transition of in- and out- of school youth to obtain employment and achieve economic self-sufficiency.]

27. Those are all the questions I have. Do you have any questions or comments about the survey?

Yes 1   → **[GO TO 27a]**
No 2   ↑
Refused .... -7   ° **[GO TO 28]**

27a.   What are your questions or comments?

_____

28. Would you be interested in receiving a report via e-mail on the results of this survey? Your e-mail address will not be associated with your completed survey.

Yes 1   → **[GO TO 28a]**
No 2   ↑
Refused .... -7   ° **[GO TO THANK]**

28a.   May I have your email address, please?

_____@_____

THANK: Thank you very much for participating in this very important survey.

Appendix C: Data Collection Procedures

CATI Telephone Procedures

Westat has five Telephone Research Center (TRC) facilities as well as at home interviewers working in secured private work environments. The TRCs are located across the continental United States, including the main TRC in Maryland, as well as additional TRCs in California, Florida, and Maryland. The at home interviewing staff spans the United States. For this study, Westat utilized interviewers to best cover all U.S time zones for the survey. In general, most calls for this study were made Monday through Friday between 9 a.m. and 5 p.m. in the respondent's time. However, if there were businesses that needed to be called in the evening or on the weekends, these were accommodated as needed. (If a business' telephone number had been disconnected, Westat did not attempt to obtain a new number, because businesses regularly close.)

Westat administered the employer questionnaire using Computer Assisted Telephone Interviewing (CATI). Westat worked closely with CESSI and ODEP to revise, format, and finalize the questionnaire for computer-assisted telephone interviewing (CATI) (minor modifications were necessary to format the questionnaire for CATI). Computer assisted telephone interviewing (CATI) provides several advantages over traditional methods of telephone data collection and preparation. Some advantages are:

- The skip pattern logic of CATI questionnaires is fully computerized so that interviewer choice in question branching is eliminated. This assures that all questions that should be answered are asked during the interview, eliminating the need to edit for un-needed responses at the end of data collection;

- Question wording choices, including the insertion of information from previous questions in the CATI survey, are performed for the interviewer by the CATI software. This assures that respondents are asked the correct, applicable questions;

- The validity checks of response codes for closed-ended questions are performed during the interview so that invalid codes cannot be entered into the data files. This saves editing time at the end of data collection, since these types of edits are pre-programmed into CATI;

- Legal ranges for continuous variables, such as ages, dates, dollar amounts, etc., are checked during the interview. This eliminates the need to edit out-of-range responses at the end of data collection;

- Consistency checking between related items is performed on line, and questions with inconsistent entries are re-asked or probed with additional questions to minimize both respondent error and interviewer entry error;

- Because so much editing is performed during data collection, the need for routine data retrieval is eliminated;

- Post-data-collection machine editing is minimized, facilitating the rapid preparation of data files for analysis; and

- Questionnaires can be designed to use special question series aimed at particular respondent subgroups, because the branching to and around these items is handled by the CATI software.

The system of CATI software used for this survey is called the Cheshire System and was developed by Westat especially for use on large government surveys that demand high standards of quality for deliverable datasets. Because the software was developed by Westat staff (as opposed to being purchased or leased from an outside source), Westat has both the legal rights and the staff capabilities to augment and modify the system whenever new features or variations are desired.

Programming the CATI

Westat programmed the paper questionnaire developed by ODEP into the CATI system. This involved

- reviewing the questionnaire;
- inserting specifications into the questionnaire;
- preparing the specifications for the CATI programmer; and
- programming and testing the questionnaire into CATI

Reviewing the questionnaire

ODEP developed the survey instrument. Westat, in consultation with CESSI, reviewed the questionnaire for wording that needed to be added to insure ease of flow on the telephone.

Inserting specifications into the questionnaire

Westat inserted specification language into the questionnaire. Skips and logic checks are specified on the electronic version of the questionnaire. Skips are programmed so that interviewers are taken to the next question based on the respondent's previous answers. Logic checks are inserted to verify answers interviewers have entered into CATI that may not make sense (e.g. respondent's number of years with company of 100 years). One "help" screen with an extended definition was programmed. It was accessible by a function key as needed by the interviewer. This screen was made known to the interviewers during training as well as by the indication of "HELP" on the applicable screen.

Preparing the specifications for the CATI programmer

The design document produced:

- **details on skips and different ways questions may need to be asked in CATI.** Details of how skips worked in the questionnaire as well as the needed question variations.
- **screen displays**. These specifications were for how the actual screens looked in CATI for each question. In addition to creating screen displays for all questions, some questions required more than one screen display. For example, if there is more than one way to ask a question (e.g. asking a question in the present tense vs. asking the question in the past tense), this would require more than one screen to be designed.

The document that is produced during this phase of CATI programming is used:

- By the programmers to program the questionnaire into CATI;
- By the testers to check if the questionnaire has been programmed;
- By the trainers to produce training materials. These specifications can have project specific comments in them, so that the trainers have additional information on what is important to emphasize during training; and
- Data preparation/editing staff use the document to make edits to the data. They are able to check in the document for the relevance of comments interviewers have added into the CATI and to upcode "other specify" responses, if needed.

The TRC also developed specifications for contact procedures for the survey. Contact procedures for this study included contacting the appropriate respondent, setting appointments for interviews, as well as specifications for other call results, such as a ring no answer or a busy signal. The TRC staff also checked the wording of the questions for grammatical errors and the specifications for syntax errors. If errors were found, they contacted project staff to update the questionnaire and the specifications.

Programming and testing the questionnaire into CATI

Once the specifications for the questionnaire were completed, they were ready for programming into CATI. As the programmer worked through the specifications, s/he needs to contact project staff for clarification. After the programming specifications were complete, the instrument was divided into questionnaire sections for programming. As each section was programmed, it underwent two rounds of code testing. First, the original programmer proofed the screen library against the screen text in the specifications, checked the data dictionary against variable definitions in the specifications, and checked the flow language programming against the skip patterns in the instrument. Once the first round of testing was completed, the section was turned over to another programmer who reproduced first round checks and assessed overall section presentation. This second round of testing resulted in recommendations for changes to screen layout, or question flow that enhanced the effectiveness of the instrument versions. All errors or recommended changes were documented on problem sheet forms that are routed to key project members for guidance, discussion, and reconciliation. After all questionnaire sections completed the two rounds of testing, the individual sections were assembled into a complete instrument. The third round of testing focused on transitions from one questionnaire section to another and on restart points to ensure that the flow between sections and topics was smooth, and that all questionnaire sections appeared in the proper sequence. The final stage of testing occurred after the first three stages of code testing were complete. Project personnel, interviewer supervisors, and programmers all participated in testing at this stage which considered screen layout, question item wording, transitions, and skip patterns.

Training interviewers

The quality of the data is directly related to the quality of the training of the interviewers. Westat thoroughly trains interviewers in all aspects of data collection, from initial contact procedures to conducting the interview to refusal avoidance and conversion. The training materials that were developed for the study's interviewers included the following:

> **Training Agenda**--The agenda documents the 4 Pre-Production Training sessions: The On-Line Self-Tutorial, WebEx 1 Session, Role Play Session, WebEx 2 Follow-Up Session. It divided the training into timed sessions on specific topics

> **Interviewers' On-Line Self-Tutorial Training and Training Materials**. The training materials document survey procedures for the interviewer and can be printed and serve as references. The on-line tutorial provides an overview of the study, along with needed question-by-question specifications for each item in each questionnaire and an introduction to the Questions and Answers for the study. All interviewers have access to an on-line application for their individual project. This provides space for memos, procedural updates, and goal charts as well as an opportunity for interviewers to comment on successes or ask questions to be answered.

> **WebEx1 Training.** The trainer acts as a respondent for many different scripted contact scenarios and 1 lengthy questionnaire scenario. The trainees take turns acting as the <u>verbal</u> respondents to these scenarios, using professional manners and techniques. As needed the trainer makes necessary comments as well as pointing out the best techniques being used by the trainees. The

trainer does control the CATI questionnaire being viewed by the trainees. However, the trainer enters the answers the trainee acting as verbal interviewer dictates. These **Interactives** help familiarize the interviewers with the questionnaire and reading the questions and categories. In addition, it provides practice in seeking the appropriate respondent, avoiding refusals, requesting re-mails of the introductory letter, handling of interim results, that is, busy signals, ring no answers, voice mails and leaving messages, appointment making. Answers to the expected **commonly asked questions and objections** are provided by the interviewers during this session and a written assignment on this is provided to reinforce refusal avoidance. A **Demonstration interview** to show the proper flow of the instrument is performed during this session with the trainer as the interviewer and the session's group leader acting as the respondent.

Role Plays—During this session, the trainees are partnered and approximately 5 sets of partners were assigned a Team Leader who would answer questions, monitor, and coach. One partner started as interviewer and the other acted as the respondent using a scripted role play book. During this session, the interviewer had control of the instrument and entered answers. These scripts require the "interviewer" partner to practice several interviewing techniques, that is, probe, avoid refusals, answer questions, make comments in the instrument appropriately, correct changed answers. For the next scripted role play, the partners reversed roles and the "interviewer" became the "respondent" and vice versa. There were 4 questionnaire role play books plus a contact role play divided into multiple scenarios for the 2 partners. The team leaders decided which trainees needed more role play practice. No interviewer was allowed to make live calls to respondents until they successfully passed this part of the training.

WebEx 2—This session reviewed the problems noted during role plays, the written question and answer exercise assigned during WebEx1, and answered any outstanding trainee questions about the instrument and study protocol.

Monitoring Data Collection Quantity

CATI Scheduler

Scheduling System. The scheduler component of the CATI system is used to manage the flow and assignment of questionnaires to interviewers. The basis for this system is a structure of queues. Each queue contains a list of assignment IDs to be interviewed. The number of queues, and the purpose of each queue, is defined by project staff prior to commencing work. For example, a simple configuration of queues would be: Ring No Answer, Busy, Callback - Appointment, Ready. Each queue has several controls associated with it that can be altered by project staff while CATI operations are under way. These are default priority, weighting factor, queue open/close time and case release time. A brief explanation of the purpose of each parameter follows:

The priority number controls the order in which queues are searched for the next ID to interview. Each queue can have a separate priority number assigned, or several queues can have the same priority. When each queue has a separate priority number, they are emptied in order from highest to lowest priority. However, when several queues have equal priority, one ID is taken from each queue in a roundtable fashion until all the queues with the same priority are empty;

The weighting factor gives the project staff additional control over the selection of queues when a group of queues has the same priority. Initially, all queues are assigned a weight of 1. If, for example, the project staff wanted to make assignments from the small business queue at 3 times the rate of the other queues, that queue would be assigned a weight of 3. This forces the scheduler to take 3 cases from the small business queue before moving on to select 1 each from the remaining queues. Altering priority numbers and weighting factors gives the project staff maximum flexibility in scheduling work assignments;

Each queue has a start and stop time that is examined by the scheduler before a potential case is selected from the queue. Queue start and stop times can be staggered across the country to follow the time zone in each area. For example, this prevents embarrassing situations where an East Coast interviewer starting at 9:00 AM contacts a California respondent at 6:00 AM.

Certain queues have a time attribute associated with each case that is examined by the scheduler before releasing the case from the queue -- for instance, the Ring No Answer, Busy, or Callback queues. The project staff may want to make adjustments to case release times for the queues depending on interviewer or data entry workload. By altering the case release times, the project staff can release work earlier than expected or postpone work until a later time.

Scheduler Operations. The Cheshire System scheduler uses a "real-time" approach to distributing work and rescheduling additional interviewing. Project staff may interactively monitor and intervene to adjust specific scheduling facets, but, in practice, this is seldom necessary. When an interviewer requires work, the program requests work from the scheduler. The scheduler process uses the priority, weight, and start/stop time of queues and the individual appointment time of interviews to select the next case available for work. When the case is next scheduled, it is determined through a rescheduling algorithm by the result of the work performed and the status of the case. This algorithm may be adjusted for specific projects. The highlights of Westat's standard algorithm include the following:

- Cases are immediately rescheduled for an appointed time when a specific appointment is made.
- Contacts without specific appointments are (1) rescheduled for the general time indicated by the respondent as good to re-contact or (2) rescheduled for a time corresponding to the original successful contact.
- Unsuccessful contacts are rotated among time slots for recontact on a calculated basis.
- Busy-tone calls are scheduled for recall in fifteen minutes.
- Firm appointments that result in non-contact are scheduled for recall in twenty minutes.

Quality Control Procedures

This survey was conducted using Computer Assisted Telephone Interviewing (CATI) software. CATI is programmed to follow skip patterns. Interviewers are trained to probe to get complete answers to all survey questions. If a respondent does not know how to answer a question, or refuses to answer a particular question, those options are allowed on the questionnaire as well. However, no question can be skipped.

For the survey, Westat implemented procedures to review and edit questionnaire responses. Westat maintains a large in-house data preparation staff experienced in performing tasks for all study types conducted at Westat. During a CATI study, data preparation staff checked the CATI responses for consistency and continuously monitored the data. Interviewer comments and problem sheets were reviewed daily and updates were made as necessary. Frequencies of responses to all data items were reviewed to ensure that appropriate skip patterns were followed by the CATI system. Each item is checked to make sure that the correct number of responses is represented. When a discrepancy was discovered, the problem cases were identified and reviewed.

Westat incorporated quality control into the design and implementation of each component of the survey. Westat views quality control as a continuous process that is integrated seamlessly into the development and conduct of the entire survey process.

Recruiting. Quality control for data collection started with a strong and sensitive staff of interviewers who read well, speak clearly on the telephone, are articulate, have good listening skills, and have an assertive but pleasant business manner.

Training. Those individuals who possess these qualities are invited to general interviewer training (GIT) where they undergo further scrutiny. This training is a self-paced on-line tutorial composed of survey information and techniques and exercises geared to target those who passed the initial screening but who are otherwise not suitable for interviewing, for example, cannot follow directions. The next step is CATI Train which, for this study, covered Westat's Cheshire system. Most mastered this quickly; those who did not were released. At this point the successful trainees were sent to project-specific training. This training, like GIT and CATI Train, is fully scripted to ensure consistency across training groups. Lead trainers' evaluate the performance of the trainees with the Group Leader. During training, the group leader completes an evaluation form for each trainee, which permits trainee performance to be ranked on factors such as reading ability, questionnaire navigation, understanding of concepts, answering respondent questions, and refusal avoidance. Monitoring sheets, which are completed on the scripted role plays, are also part of the trainee evaluation. Those who do not successfully complete training are released.

Production. Standard quality control procedures include systematic and rigorous monitoring of telephone interviewer performance throughout the telephone data collection field period. This silent monitoring is from secure audio-visual stations on site and in homes of team leaders. The monitoring rate was the highest at the beginning of data collection and was higher for new interviewers than for experienced interviewers. All monitoring was documented on a Monitoring Document Form and feedback given immediately to the interviewer. Monitoring forms for each interview were reviewed weekly by the TRC supervisory staff and any interviewers who were identified as in need of additional monitoring were monitored more heavily the following week. Reinforcement coaching was carried out as needed. In addition, a project coordinator reviewed monitoring sheets to identify common problems across interviewers that might reveal the need for additional training. Team leaders also answered questions interviewers had during interviews. Production, refusal, attendance, and attrition rates were monitored, also. Weekly interviewer meetings, on-line memoranda and bulletin board postings kept the interviewers apprised of procedural modifications, response counts and increases by industry and size, and other project activities. Any discrepancies or mailing errors were quickly identified by staff and discussed with the associated interviewers.

Data editing. The CATI program's edit checks ensured that during the course of each interview, non-contradictory data or data within reasonable ranges would be entered as responses to the survey questions. In addition, after completion of the surveys, computer-assisted editing was performed to ensure data consistency; reconcile hierarchical database segments (e.g., if the answer to one question requires that there be a specific response to another); identify outliers, and range edits through the use of Westat's range verification utility that passes all response entries through the data dictionary range specifications and produces a report flagging all items that exceed the range; and verify the completeness of each finalized case.

Frequencies of responses to open-ended and other/specify responses were also run. These responses were reviewed and were either upcoded into existing response categories (for other/specify responses) or categories were developed (for both open-ended and other/specify responses) for analysis. Cases in which the industry type changed were reviewed to determine that the industry remained in scope. A few cases where the industry was coded agricultural and a utility company were changed from a complete to ineligible status.

Screening and Recruiting Respondents

We contacted the selected companies and conducted a 15 minute telephone interview with the senior executives knowledgeable about company policies and practices on recruiting, hiring, retaining and advancing employees with disabilities. This activity began after OMB clearance, and once the pilot study was completed. Westat employed appropriate telephone interviewing methods to insure cooperation of senior executives for this short survey.

The research team's extensive experience with business surveys has shown that response rates are maximized when procedures for achieving them are designed into and executed at every stage of a study's implementation. These procedures began with the plan for development of the sample frame and continued through the development of the questionnaire and data collection. Factors that specifically influence reluctant individuals to participate include the following:

Advance Letter. An introductory letter was sent to sampled businesses. The letter was on ODEP letterhead and signed by an official at ODEP. The goal of this letter was to introduce the study, emphasize confidentiality, explain respondent's rights, and alert the respondents that an interviewer will be calling. A toll-free number was included so that respondents could call to verify the legitimacy of the study, to ask questions or to set up an appointment for an interview.

Contacting the most appropriate respondent. Westat sent all small and medium-sized businesses the advance letter prior to the interviewer's call. Large businesses were called to obtain the name of the most senior knowledgeable respondent. That respondent was then sent the advance letter. Once the letter was sent, an interviewer called to complete the interview. If we could not speak with that respondent, we then determined the name of another knowledgeable respondent. We asked for respondents by title, using the titles cited in the questionnaire. In a large company, many of the questions on the survey were referred to Human Resources for responses. Large companies often have human resources employees who are responsible for recruiting employees with disabilities and tracking accommodations made for employees.

Contacting the corporate headquarters. Westat contacted the business' corporate headquarters, if applicable, and tried to interview a respondent at the corporate office. If this was not possible, Westat then conducted the interview with a senior knowledgeable respondent at one of the company's locations.

Experienced executive interviewers. Westat has a dedicated staff of experienced, executive interviewers whose job it is to conduct interviews with senior level business executives.

Interviewers' ability to obtain cooperation. Westat uses experienced and well trained interviewers. All interviewers were monitored, evaluated, and provided with instant feedback on their performance to eliminate interaction patterns or telephone demeanor that might be detrimental to achieving cooperation. (Newer interviewers were monitored at a higher rate than experienced interviewers.)

Flexibility in scheduling interviews. Being available to speak with people when it is most convenient for them is sometimes overlooked as a factor that can tip the balance in favor of cooperation for an individual who has doubts about participating. Interviewing activities for the survey were scheduled to coincide with the hours people are most likely to be at work. In the event the respondents needed to schedule interviews for a particular time, the CATI system accommodated their needs. Special arrangements were made for those respondents available to be interviewed only on a weekend or in the evening as staff was generally scheduled only Monday through Friday 9 a.m. – 5 p.m. in Eastern through Pacific time zones.

Well-worded introductory statement. Our telephone interviewing experience has shown that one of the main reasons for nonresponse is that respondents hang up before the interviewer has a chance to explain the study. Immediately reassuring the person answering the telephone that the interviewer is not a salesperson and that the study was being done for the Department of Labor was crucial to the respondent's decision to listen to the rest of the introduction.

Refusal avoidance and refusal conversion. Perhaps the most significant technique for persuading reluctant individuals to participate is the interviewer training segment that encourages respondent participation. Nearly as important is a well-planned and concerted effort to convert each refusal to final cooperation. For each case in which the respondent refused to participate, the interviewer completed a Non-Interview Response Form (NIRF). The form captured information about key characteristics of the refusing respondent and the stated reason(s) for refusing to participate. Special interviewer training sessions were led by highly experienced supervisors for a select group of interviewers. The sessions included participating in the analysis of survey-specific and generic reasons for refusal, preparing answers and statements that are responsive to the objections; effective use of voice and manner on the telephone, and role-playing of different situations. This team of customer cooperation interviewers re-contacted the reluctant respondents.

Penetrating companies with difficult access. Four interviewers were trained in various ways to reach wanted respondents when an IVR system allowed no access without an individual's name and/or extension or when company policy prohibited the operator from transferring a call without a name or extension. This required use of the Internet, specifically Googling the company or a general phone directory site which sometimes would include key employee names and direct telephone numbers. The training consisted of periodic sharing of verbal phrases that produced the best results in breaking through these company barriers.

Interviewer Debriefing Report

The interviewers noted the following problem areas:

Errors or Outdated Information in Sample. These included individual names that never had a business of any kind and individuals who had not been in business for many years.

Questions. A request was made that questions in future questionnaires be more explicit and less confusing to the respondent. For this, probably a larger pretest would have been needed. The primary examples given were:

> **Question 1.** We show that you have [NUMBER] employees. Is that correct? [IF NEEDED: Please count all employees, not just full time employees.] Respondents

employed by companies with more than 1 location tended to say no, thinking only of their location or division or asked if that was "just here or all branches?" So, the interviewers felt that part of Q2 should have been incorporated in Q1: "Including any corporate headquarters, subsidiaries, and branches, we show that you have [NUMBER] employees. Is that correct?"

Question 14. Would any of the following types of information persuade you to recruit people with a disability? What about ... There was a general impression that smaller and non-profit companies tended to be impatient with many in this set of questions because they considered the options to be geared toward larger companies.

Many respondents perceived the questions as being repetitive. Although training emphasized the need to stress the words hiring, retaining, advancing, the interviewers offered two suggestions for future interviews with this type questioning. (1) Ask the question, and then ask the effect on hiring, retaining, advancing or (2) Have a preface indicating that the following series of questions are going to be asked about hiring and then about retaining, and then about advancing employees with disabilities. The first set is about hiring. Then when you reach retaining, state: "The next questions are about retaining employees with disabilities. We have found that sometimes companies have the same answers as for hiring but others have different answers. We appreciate your input on this." Then use the same approach for a preface on advancing people with disabilities.

Contacting the Correct Respondent. The interviewers stated that this was the number one challenge. Company policies and Interactive Voice Response systems have increased the inability to reach designated respondents in the most timely fashion. The large firms were the most difficult to interview because many used automated voice mail systems that were very difficult to penetrate and key employees were well protected by their staff.